D1325589

MODERN LEGAL STUDIES

COMPENSATION FOR UNEMPLOYMENT

AUSTRALIA
The Law Book Company Ltd.
Sydney : Melbourne : Brisbane

CANADA AND U.S.A.
The Carswell Company Ltd.
Agincourt, Ontario

INDIA
N.M. Tripathi Private Ltd.
Bombay

ISRAEL
Steimatzky's Agency Ltd.
Jerusalem : Tel Aviv : Haifa

MALAYSIA : SINGAPORE : BRUNEI
Malayan Law Journal (Pte.) Ltd.
Singapore

NEW ZEALAND
Sweet & Maxwell (N.Z.) Ltd.
Wellington

PAKISTAN
Pakistan Law House
Karachi

MODERN LEGAL STUDIES

COMPENSATION
FOR
UNEMPLOYMENT

by

JOHN MESHER,
B.A., B.C.L.(Oxon), LL.M.(Yale)

*of Gray's Inn, Barrister; Lecturer in Laws
at Queen Mary College, London*

LONDON
SWEET & MAXWELL
1976

Published in 1976 by
Sweet & Maxwell Ltd. of
11 New Fetter Lane, London.
Photoset by Red Lion Setters, London
Printed in Great Britain by
Fletcher & Son Ltd., Norwich

ISBN Hardback 0 421 20340 4
Paperback 0 421 20350 1

PREFACE

This is a short book on a large subject. As such it can act as only an introduction to the legal issues involved in the process of obtaining compensation for unemployment. It has also to be primarily a law book. I have excluded, for instance, the practice established by Industrial Tribunals in favour of a fuller discussion of the legal framework controlling it. I have also treated topics somewhat unevenly, trying to give more space to less readily accessible topics, such as decisions of the National Insurance Commissioners. I have written with law students particularly in mind, both labour law students and the increasing numbers studying welfare or social security law. I hope, however, that the book may be useful to practitioners and others who have, unfortunately, to advise more and more people who have lost their jobs.

Most references have been incorporated into the text, so that there are no footnotes. Books and articles are cited briefly by the author's name; the full references appear at the end of the book. For the uninitiated I should explain the citation of National Insurance Commissioners' Decisions. Citations prefixed by R (U) (*e.g.* R (U) 20/64) are to reported decisions on unemployment benefit, which are published by the Stationery Office. Citations prefixed by C.U. (*e.g.* C.U. 16/73) are to "numbered" decisions, which are available for public inspection at the Commissioners' offices.

I have incurred many debts of gratitude over the long

gestation period of this book. Perhaps I can single out two of the many colleagues and students at Queen Mary College who have, wittingly or unwittingly, helped me. First, Reuben Hasson, now Professor of Law at Osgoode Hall Law School, who was a constant source of encouragement, and secondly, my wife Hilary, who has been of immense help at every stage. Finally, I must mention the publishers, who have borne the seemingly endless revision called for by new legislation with a good deal more patience than I did.

July 1976   JOHN MESHER

CONTENTS

OTHER BOOKS IN THE SERIES:

TABLE OF CASES

ix

Table of Cases

Table of Cases

Table of Cases

TABLE OF DECISIONS

Table of Decisions

TABLE OF STATUTES

Chapter 1

INTRODUCTION

Unemployment in Great Britain is big business. Not as big as some other areas of welfare expenditure, but still substantial. In the third quarter of 1975 over £96 million was paid out in unemployment benefit, with at least half as much again in supplementary benefit, to the unemployed. In the same period over £55 million in redundancy payments was paid, as well as unknown amounts for wrongful or unfair dismissal. Despite this scale of expenditure unemployment is not a pleasant prospect. The number of unemployed is a constant object of social concern; their condition is often thought to merit particular sympathy. Many of the estimated 10 million whose jobs come to an end each year need no assistance, for about 65-70 per cent. of these terminations are voluntary. Nonetheless, large numbers of people suffer unemployment for short periods, find a job and leave the registers, to be replaced by others. The turnover both of vacancies and of those registered for employment is quite high (D.E. Gazette, September 1974, p.302). The plight of the longer term unemployed is more serious. Increases in the volume of unemployment result as much from people remaining out of work longer as from more people losing their jobs. On October 9, 1975, 61.3 per cent. of the 1,033,340 unemployed (excluding school leavers and adult students) had been registered for more than eight weeks. At the same time more than 160,000 had been unemployed for over a year. On

October 14, 1974, 57.7 per cent. had been registered for more than eight weeks and 127,720 for more than a year. Since hardship can be expected to increase the longer unemployment lasts, fears of rising figures are quite justified. Any unemployed person has a real interest in the financial benefits available to him. This provides my first focus. Benefits are described from the point of view of the unemployed person claiming them (for simplicity I call this person "the claimant" throughout).

There are other reasons for interest in provision for unemployment. Society regards unemployment as a considerable evil. In a society where the work ethic is potent and where most people's lives revolve around and are shaped by their jobs this is not surprising. Hence the complex range of benefits, recently extended, that seek to help those without work. However, it is the corollary of the work ethic that the natural state of man is idleness. The work ethic is necessary because otherwise people would slip into the delights of sloth, which are inherently more attractive than those of work ("the Devil makes work for idle hands"). Therefore, society must take care to save people from the temptations of natural sin. The tension between compassion and generosity on the one hand and the aims of social control on the other is evident in most social welfare programmes (and needs much more than this crude summary to be properly worked out), but appears at its sharpest in the peculiarly sensitive area of unemployment. What is particularly interesting is how social control is applied to differing groups, as defined by the kind of benefit they are claiming.

I hope that these general issues will be illuminated in the chapters stating the law. I have not illustrated them at every point, but have tried to pull the strands together in the Conclusion. The intervening chapters are mainly straightforward statements of the law, with a few criticisms of particular illogicalities or unfairnesses. Each chapter deals with a decision common to all the benefits described. Coverage describes the broad class of people potentially eligible for each, with some discussion of financing to complete the overall structure. The next chapter, Dismissal and Unemployment, deals with the precise contingency that gives rise to compensation, whether it is dismissal, unemployment or some combination. The chapter on The Reason for Termination of Employment covers two distinct areas. The first is how far certain benefits are available only to claimants who show that they have been dismissed for a particular reason, *e.g.* redundancy. The more general issue is how claimants who can be said to have brought unemployment on themselves (including by misconduct) are disqualified. Benefits covers the compensation available and how the various schemes are co-ordinated. The concern with voluntary unemployment is continued in Neglect of Job Opportunities, which describes how the claimant's conduct while unemployed may disqualify him. I do not deal at all with the effect of trade disputes on benefits. This important topic is too complex to be contained within this book and raises many issues of its own.

Within each chapter, benefits are described in the same order, starting with those coming wholly from the employer, ending with that coming wholly from general taxation. Thus common law damages for wrongful dismissal come first, followed by compensation for unfair dismissal payable under the Trade Union and Labour Relations Act 1974. Next comes the curious mixture of redundancy payments, under the Redundancy Payments Act 1965. Finally come the two social security benefits. Unemployment benefit is regulated by the National Insurance Act 1965 and from January 1, 1977, the Social Security Act 1975. (This division is the result of my reading of regulation 3 of the Social Security (Short-Term Benefits) (Transitional) Regulations 1974, but the government seems to assume that only the contribution conditions of the old law survive for claims after April 1975.) Unemployment benefit comes mainly from National Insurance (now Social Security) contributions. Finally, supplementary benefit is paid under the Supplementary Benefit Act 1966 from general taxation.

Readers will have noticed a number of sources of financial support missing from this list, notably private severance payments or "golden handshakes," refunds of pension contributions or early payment of occupational pensions, and income tax rebates. They are omitted not because they are unimportant, but because the description of their legal control cannot easily be split up to fit into the following chapters. Therefore, I say something about them here.

Private Severance Payments

These are the various kinds of payments made by employers to departing employees outside statutory obligations or ordinary contract damages. Precise information is hard to come by in this area. There are some private redundancy schemes more generous than the statutory one. These tend to be in the public sector. But W.W. Daniel's national survey found that only 6 per cent. of a sample of unemployed received a redundancy payment separate from the statutory one (Daniel, p.117). Occasionally, provision for a severance payment in wider circumstances is written into a contract, but, since this has tax disadvantages, most golden handshakes are paid without legal obligation. They are more common to management and executives than to manual workers. Thus while 5 per cent. of all unemployed received such a payment, the figure for the managerial/professional group was 10 per cent. This group was also more likely to receive a non-statutory redundancy payment: 13 per cent. of them did (*ibid.*).

There is seldom any legal problem about making payments. The only doubt is whether companies can make *ex gratia* payments. *Parke* v. *Daily News Ltd*. [1962] Ch. 927 held that when a business was about to close down the distribution of the proceeds of the sale of its goodwill to its redundant employees was *ultra vires*. The payments could not be for the benefit of the company, *i.e.* the shareholders. While a business is a going concern, however, payments to ex-employees can usually be said to benefit the company by attracting and keeping other employees.

Payments usually do not depend on formal distinctions between dismissal and voluntary leaving, and a wide definition of redundancy may be adopted. In redundancy schemes the amount of payments often varies according to length of service and current earnings. Similar factors tend to influence amounts of severance payments though in a less formal way. Long service may be rewarded by a higher payment, and an easy calculation is to pay so many months' salary on top of that in lieu of notice. It is hard to say how often misconduct results in the loss of a payment. Of course then there may not be dismissal for redundancy, but in a wider context employers may pay a misbehaving employee as a quick and convenient way of getting rid of him. Similarly, most payments cannot be affected by subsequent failures to find work. Until 1961, lump sum payments were generally not subject to tax. Exceptions were (1) if the payment is in consideration for entering a restrictive covenant, higher, but not basic, rate tax is payable (Income and Corporation Taxes Act 1970, s.34); (2) if the payment is in pursuance of an existing arrangement, or in anticipation of future services, it is taxable. Concern about large tax-free golden handshakes led to the provision in the Finance Act 1960 that any payment made in connection with the termination of employment, if not already taxable, is subject to tax in the recipient's hands (ss.37-38, Sched.13; now sections 187-188 of the Income and Corporation Taxes Act). Amounts up to £5,000 are exempt from tax, although payments from all sources (including statutory redundancy payments and compensation for unfair dismissal) must be added together for this purpose. Any payment the employer makes can be deducted from his profits chargeable to corporation tax etc., provided that it is for the purposes of trade. Thus the exchequer can be said to make a contribution to the payment in the form of tax foregone.

Pensions

Employees who are members of contributory pension schemes nearly always have the right on leaving employment to a refund of their past contributions, sometimes with interest. However, the benefit of schemes is distributed rather unequally. In 1970, 75 per cent. of non-manual men were members, compared with 46 per cent. of manual men. The corresponding figures for women were 47 per cent. and 18 per cent. (Social Trends No.3, Table 44). Between a quarter and a third of schemes were non-contributory, with this being slightly more common in non-manual schemes (Report of the Government Actuary, p.21). The amount received obviously varies according to the level of contribution, so can be substantial. Tax is deducted by the employer from the refund.

The ability to take a refund is limited from April 6, 1975, by the Social Security Act 1973. Schedule 16, para.6 secures that anyone over 25 who leaves a scheme after at least five years' membership must have his benefits under the scheme preserved until retirement. The right to take a refund of contributions made before April 1975 remains. The new rule may be for the member's own good in the long run (although this depends on the way the pension is calculated), but it does deprive him of what might be useful capital. Schemes are free to make their own rules for members leaving after less than five years, so can restrict refunds in all circumstances. Employers may only pay the benefit of their contributions to an early leaver at the cost of the scheme's not being recognised by the Revenue for the purposes of tax allowances on contributions.

Pensions may provide a useful income for those who are prematurely retired, when an occupational pension may be paid early. In the Daniel survey 18 per cent. of the over-55s said that they had retired (p.53), and at least 75 per cent. of these were receiving pensions (p.55). Managerial and professional groups were particularly prominent: 51 per cent. of this group over 55 had retired (p.54).

Income Tax Rebates

PAYE tax is calculated on the assumption that the taxpayer will continue to be employed at the same wage throughout the tax year. If wages cease, as during unemployment, this means that too much tax has been paid, so that a rebate is payable. If the taxpayer has not given up employment altogether, a rebate is paid after four weeks' unemployment. Rebates are subsequently calculated every four weeks until the taxpayer starts work again or has recovered all the tax he has paid in that tax year. The amount for a single man currently works out at about £4.50 a week and for a married man with no children at about £6.40. The more tax that has been paid, because of higher earnings, the longer rebates will be paid, but the major determinant is the timing of unemployment in the tax year. If it is near the beginning little tax will have been paid, so that rebates will not last long.

Chapter 2

COVERAGE AND FINANCING

Here the concern is with the definition of the class of people potentially protected and with the way compensation is paid for. The problems are thus large-scale.

Wrongful Dismissal

Anyone who provides services under a contract may sue for breach of contract if it is terminated prematurely. There are special rules applying to employees, but independent contractors, apprentices, etc. have their contract protection, such as it is. There are one or two small exceptions to this generality. Those employed by minors in other than a domestic or personal capacity might have problems, but this must be a minute class. More numerous are Crown servants. Whether they work under a contract or not, it is clear that they may legally be dismissed at will (see *Riordan* v. *War Office* [1961] 1 W.L.R. 210).

Any damages paid for wrongful dismissal are obviously part of the costs of the employer's business. As such they are no doubt paid ultimately by the consumers of the employer's products or services. It is unlikely that they would come out of profits, although it is noteworthy that payments made may be claimed as business expenses to diminish the amount of tax paid on profits. Thus one may regard the government as contributing the amount of tax saved.

Unfair Dismissal

The Trade Union and Labour Relations Act 1974, Sched.1, para.4(1) provides that "in every employment to which this section applies every employee shall have the right not to be dismissed by his employer." An employee is someone who works under a contract of service (s.30). Thus independent contractors are excluded and it is necessary to say a little about how to tell the difference, especially as coverage for redundancy and unemployment benefit depends on the same distinction.

The National Industrial Relations Court (NIRC) did not get past saying that you can tell an employee when you see one (*Challinor* v. *Taylor* [1972] I.C.R. 129). Such an unprincipled approach leads to chaos and the courts have in other contexts developed a number of tests. The same test seems to be used whatever statute is concerned, though it may be that the way it is applied varies with the context. The full arguments for the eclipse of the tests based on control by the employer or integration into the employer's business are in the textbooks. The accepted modern test is some variety of the "multiple" test. The break came with the decision of MacKenna J. in *Ready-Mixed Concrete Ltd*. v. *Minister of Pensions and National Insurance* [1968] 2 Q.B. 497. He rejected the integration test and while keeping some degree of control as necessary for the existence of a contract of service he took account of a large number of factors in deciding that the man in question was more like a small businessman than an employee. He was a driver who owned his lorry, and whose earnings depended on his efficiency (*i.e.* miles driven) and financial investment. This outweighed the fact that both he and the lorry were in Ready-Mixed uniform, it was being bought on HP from an associated company of Ready-Mixed, and that he undertook to obey orders "as if he was an employee." One may have serious doubts about the correctness of the decision itself, but the approach of looking at the alleged employee's activities and asking if he is in business on his own account has been accepted and extended. It was put in this form by Cooke J. in *Market Investigations Ltd*. v. *Minister of Social Security* [1969] 2 Q.B. 173. Control was merely one factor, but also to be considered were "whether the man performing the services provides his own equipment, whether he hires his own helpers, what degree of financial risk he takes, what degree of responsibility for investment and management he has, and whether and how far he has an opportunity of profiting from sound management in the performance of his task" (at p.184). The same approach was taken by the Divisional Court in *Construction Industry Training Board* v. *Labour Force Ltd*. [1970] 3 All E.R. 220 and the emphasis on the open-ended list of factors and their varying weight in differing circumstances reinforced. Again the factual decision is open to challenge, especially reliance in the *Labour Force* case on the arrangement adopted by the parties for National Insurance Contributions and tax and their own description of their relationship. Some courts appear to have more regard for the contractual formalities than the economic realities : the National Insurance scheme has had to be amended to nullify the effect of the last two decisions.

Nonetheless, the test is finally established by Lord Widgery C.J. in *Global Plant Ltd*. v. *Secretary of State for Health and Social Security* [1972] 1 Q.B. 139. Its major characteristic is its flexibility. This carries the dangers of slipping into the purely impressionistic test and of offering more scope for employers and workers who wish to evade the many responsibilities that go with the contract of service. The remedy here is no doubt specific regulations such as those adopted for National Insurance and (unsuccessfully) for tax purposes in the building trade. The advantage lies in the recognition that particular factors have different weight according to circumstances. This allows courts to take account of the purpose of the statute they are dealing with. The statutes dealt with in the *Labour Force* case are designed to take a levy towards a fund to promote training from all who use labour in a particular industry. A narrow definition here detracts from the objects of the Act. In considering the employer's vicarious liability in tort, control may be particularly important. On the other hand where the statutory scheme concerns the loss of a job, the severance of a relation of economic dependency, the presence or absence of control has no effect on the risk of that loss occurring and other factors may be much more important (see Asia, at p.83). These are economic realities that courts should be sensitive to, but they seem to be largely ignored in the reported decisions. However, the opportunity is there. How should such sensitiveness be applied to the unfair dismissal legislation? The self-employed in general are not in such a dependent relation to their employer as the employee. They are not tied by duties of fidelity, etc. and being in business on one's own account means accepting the risks of loss of contracts as well as hope of profits. They are more likely to be able to bargain at arm's length. Nonetheless, some who appear formally as independent contractors may be as dependent as any employee. The courts should not be ready to exclude such people from coverage.

Perhaps the best explanation of the need for protection against the destruction of a job is in the Donovan Report (Donovan, para.526):

"In reality people build much of their lives around their jobs. Their incomes and prospects for the future are inevitably founded in the expectation that their jobs will continue. For workers in many situations dismissal is a disaster. For some workers it may make inevitable the breaking up of a community and the uprooting of homes and families. Others, and particularly older workers, may be faced with the greatest difficulty in getting work at all. The statutory provision for redundancy goes some way to recognise what is really at stake for an employee when his job is involved, but it is no less at stake if he is being dismissed for alleged incompetence or for misconduct than if he is being dismissed for redundancy. To this it is no answer that good employers will dismiss employees only if they have no alternative. Not all employers are good employers. Even if the employer's intentions are good, is it certain that his subordinates' intentions are always also good? And even when all concerned in management act in good faith, are they always necessarily right? Should their view of the case automatically prevail over the employee's?''

Donovan gives some content to the abstract phrase "job property." Though the Trade Union and Labour Relations Act, like the Redunancy Payments Act 1965, fails to prevent the destruction of this property, it goes some way to compensate for it.

Bearing this in mind, some of the statutory exclusions are hard to justify. Those over 65 (60 for women) or the normal retiring age in the undertaking are excluded (Sched.1, para.10). These are the ages at which entitlement to the National Insurance retirement pension begins and also at which entitlement to a redundancy payment stops. The argument is that after this age a person has no expectation that his job will continue. This plainly is not so for many employees as was recognised by the NIRC in considering the normal retiring age in the undertaking in *Ord* v. *Maidstone Hospital* [1974] I.C.R. 369. It was emphasised that this was not equivalent to "pensionable age." No doubt it would have looked odd to be out of step with the redundancy scheme, but the overall situation can only rest on a policy decision that the old are to make way for the young. Their dismissal is always to be fair.

Originally, 104 weeks' continuous employment with the employer were necessary to qualify for compensation. The NJAC in their Report on Dismissals Procedures had recommended a six month period, while Donovan (para.555) favoured no limits here, nor, incidentally, for age. The Trade Union and Labour Relations Act (Sched.1, para.10) now provides that the period is 26 weeks. Weeks now count for this purpose only if the employee is employed for at least 21 hours or under a contract normally involving at least 21 hours' employment (Contracts of Employment Act 1972, Sched.1, para.4). The Employment Protection Act 1975 (Sched.16, Part II, para.13) substitutes 16 hours for 21 hours. There is further relaxation in that (1) continuity is not broken if the contract hours drop to eight for a period of up to 26 weeks and (2) a claimant whose contract normally involves eight hours' employment is covered after five years' continuous employment (para.14).

Thus more part-timers will be included when this part of the Act is brought into force. This is right, for part-timers do not always have little stake in their job or work merely for pocket money. They can also be disabled, widowed or wives working to keep a family over the breadline. The fact that work is not full-time can be taken into account in deciding the fairness of dismissal.

The Employment Protection Act removes most of the other objectionable exclusions, such as that of undertakings with less than four employees. Registered dock workers, share fishermen, those ordinarily working outside Great Britain and those employed by their spouse are the groups still excluded by paragraph 9 of Schedule 1 to the Trade Union and Labour Relations Act. Anyone employed for a fixed term of at least two years is allowed to agree in writing to exclude his rights to compensation on the expiry of the term (para.12). The Court of Appeal, in the redundancy context, has held that a term is only fixed if the employer has no right to terminate the contract prematurely by notice (*BBC* v. *Ioannou* [1975] I.C.R. 267). Crown employees are specifically included by paragraph 33.

The whole of any compensation is paid by the employer, just like damages.

Redundancy Payments

The Redundancy Payments Act applies to employees, defined as for unfair dismissals, with a similar old age exclusion and a requirement of 104 weeks' continuous employment over the age of 18 for coverage. The exclusions here have more relation to the purposes of the Act, if the major purpose is seen to be encouraging the acceptance of redundancy by employees without challenge to management's decision.

Two years' employment is said to be "long enough for the worker to have begun to build up a measure of security in his job and to have proved himself a satisfactory employee in the eyes of his employer" (Ellis and McCarthy, p.6). No doubt a certain amount of attachment to a particular job has to be shown before compensation has to be given for its loss, and administrative reasons again press against allowing a large number of small claims. Quite why a worker should have to prove himself satisfactory is not clear. However, a great many jobs last less than two years already. There is a large group of workers for whom frequent changes of job are already a fact of industrial life. They scarcely need encouragement to be mobile. Further, they are the least likely to be protected by a union operating the traditional last in, first out rule. It is the long service employee who places a high value on security, and is the beneficiary of the last in, first out rule, who must be persuaded to accept the "necessity" of redundancy. Possibly the same arguments apply to the exclusion of those over retirement age; there is less compunction in disposing of the old when they have their pension to fall back on. Ellis and McCarthy (p.6) say that to give redundancy payments would create invidious distinctions between those dismissed for redundancy and others whose circumstances are the same. Since the Act creates the same distinctions for the preretirement population, the answer must rest again with the decision that the old should not expect to be re-employed, and so save the dislocation and costs of finding a new job. The wasting asset of their job property has wasted away. At the other end of the age-scale, no one under 20 is covered. The young were expected to be more mobile.

Part-timers are excluded, although the Employment Protection Act relaxations apply here also. So also are the self-employed. The hazard the redundancy scheme deals with is a change in business requirements. This is a risk that someone in business on his own account has to accept: if he chooses a declining business that is hard luck. But once again if there is a relation of economic dependency the courts should be slow to decide that a man has in fact accepted such risks. The distinction has only arisen occasionally in this context. There have been a few problems with "one-man companies." Taxi-drivers who do not own their cabs but pay a proportion of the take to the owner, who pays for maintenance, have been held to be self-employed, although not on any very clear principle (*Hill* v. *Barrie* [1967] I.T.R. 206, *Challinor* v. *Taylor* [1972] I.C.R. 129).

More detailed exclusions are provided in sections 16, 17 and 19 of the Act, and are much the same as for unfair dismissals. Those employed on fixed term contracts for over two years are allowed to agree to exclude their rights to any payment (s.15(2)), but Crown servants are not included.

The financing of the redundancy payment is somewhat odd. The initial payment comes from the employer, who then claims a rebate of 50 per cent. from the Redundancy Fund. The Fund is made up of contributions from the employers of anyone over the age of 18. The argument for using employer contributions is that industry as a whole will benefit from encouraging the mobility and efficient use of labour. In the earlier years of the scheme the rebate formula was different and the Fund had to take money from general taxation in order to meet its commitments. However, after the introduction of the present formula in 1969 the burden again falls on employers as a whole. One may again doubt how far employers, rather than the community at large in fact bear this burden, but the principle that the employer who makes a man redundant should be relieved of a substantial proportion of the cost is established. Further, the employer's 50 per cent. of the payment counts as a tax expense, as does the weekly contribution, so the community at least contributes in tax foregone.

Unemployment Benefit

Coverage is based in general on the contract of service. The precise definition of the class whose contributions count for these purposes was changed by the Social Security Act 1973. Previously, under the National Insurance Act 1965, contributions as an employed person, *i.e.* "gainfully occupied in employment ..., being employment under a contract of service" (s.1(2)(*a*)) were necessary. From April 6, 1975, the phrases are "employed earner" and "gainfully employed ... either under a contract of service" or in an office where emoluments are taxed under PAYE (Social Security Act 1975, s.2(1)(*a*)). There seems to be little difference of substance between these definitions, although now the surrounding regulations providing for special cases have been much simplified.

The self-employed are excluded. The argument is that only an employed person has anything to lose and that it would be very difficult to tell when a self-employed person was not working, for he defines his own workload. Beveridge in his Report on Social Insurance and Allied Services recognised that "there are certain classes of persons who are not technically under a contract of service but work in effect for employers (*e.g.* manual labour contractors, out-workers and private nurses)'' and said that the possibility of including them in the class of employed persons for insurance purposes should be explored (para.314). The justification for extension is greater here than in other areas, for the risk is a more general one and the result is only that people are forced to contribute for their own protection. Eligibility conditions exist to exclude from benefit those not attached to the labour force.

The authorities have in fact tried to distinguish the "real" self-employed from those who work in effect for employers by regulation. The pre-April 1975 rules (codified in the National Insurance (Classification) Regulations 1972) were very complex, but the new rules are more straightforward, possibly because the self-employed are now subject to an earnings-related levy. Under the Social Security (Categorisation of Earners) Regulations 1975, those employed by various close relatives for domestic purposes are exempted from contributions. The most important inclusion is of workers like those concerned in the *Labour Force* case. There Labour Force supplied workers to contractors for a continuing fee and the workers were held to be employed by no one. Now if the worker renders personal service to and is subject to the right of control by A, is supplied by B, and his earnings are paid by or in accordance with arrangements made with B, he is treated as an employed earner (Sched.1, Part I). Exceptions are made for home-workers, models, entertainers, etc. and for those introduced to an employer for a single fee by an agency. B is regarded as the employer and made liable for contributions accordingly (Sched.1, Part II). This provision (introduced in 1971) is a welcome control, not only over the evasions of responsibility involved in the "lump" system, but more generally over the activities of agencies supplying workers.

The requirement of "gainful" employment seems to add little in this context, if it is interpreted in the same way as the old words. It has been held to be irrelevant that the expenses of employment exceed the income received (*Vandyk* v. *Minister of Pensions and National Insurance* [1955] 1 Q.B. 29) and the contract need not provide for any remuneration, so long as some payment (*e.g.* expenses, as in *Re J.B. Griffiths, Quinn & Co.* [1968] 5 K.I.R. 128) is received for services under the contract. Further, the method of calculating contributions ensures that very low-paid employees are excluded. Apart from these classes, it should be noted that married women and people over the minimum retirement age do not need to pay the full contribution. The married woman's option will cease on April 6, 1977, except for those already opted out at that date (Social Security Pensions Act 1975, s.3).

Contributions are made by employers and employees, while the government adds 18 per cent. of the contribution income to make up the National Insurance Fund. From April 6, 1975, contributions are completely earnings-related. They are a percentage (5.5 per cent. for the employee, 8.5 per cent. for the employer: 1975 Act, s.4(6)) of all earnings up to an upper limit. This was set in the 1973 Act at £48 per week, while liability for contributions was only to arise if at least £8 was earned. These amounts will be raised periodically to approximate to 1½ and ¼ of average male earnings, and for 1975-76 are set at £69 and £11. Contributions will be collected in the same way as PAYE tax, but a distinct fund is retained. This is almost all that survives of the original Beveridge contribution system. A flat rate of contribution irrespective of income was one of the Report's fundamental principles. Those with higher incomes were to pay more only so far as they paid more tax (Beveridge, para.305). The first breach occurred in 1959 when graduated pension contributions were levied in addition to the basic contribution. These were extended when earnings-related benefits were introduced in 1966 and have since been a useful method of increasing revenue to pay for current benefits.

There seems to be no empirical evidence about who finally pays the National Insurance contributions under the British system. Even theoretical discussion comes to few firm conclusions, but opinion tends to the view that contributions are in the long run paid by labour. See, for example, J.H. Richardson: "In the long run, after time has elapsed for the processes of shifting to be completed, there will usually be no difference from the economic point of view whether the contributions are paid wholly by the employers, wholly by the workers, or are divided between them either equally or in some other proportion. The contributions are so closely related to wates that if they are paid wholly or largely by employers, wages will be correspondingly lower, and if they are paid wholly or largely by the workers, wage rates will be higher" (Richardson, p.62). If the worker's share was abolished and merged into the employer's one would not expect employers to make up the difference: in substance nothing has changed (Brittain, p.114). Thus a potential benefit is taken from the worker, but as always it is the consumer of the employer's goods or services who actually provides the income. It is true that price increases decrease real wages, but consumers are now everybody, and not everybody is a worker. It may be that in the short term employers may not be able to pass on increases in their contributions to consumers. This depends on the competitiveness of their market, particularly if capital intensive products are in competition with labour intensive. This is a general point which applies to all employers' expenditure discussed in this book, in that firms with a lot of workers compared with their competitors are at a disadvantage. However, over the long term it is unlikely that the cost of employers' contributions comes out of profits. A further complication is that the employers' contribution is allowed as a business expense for tax purposes. The result is an increase in the government's share of the Fund. The worker is taxed on his contribution. What is clear is that the major effect of dividing the contribution is a psychological one: to inculcate a feeling of joint responsibility.

It is not enough that a claimant of benefit belongs to the class that has to pay contributions. He has to have had a sufficient record of contributions in the past. The rationale is that unemployment benefit is a social insurance benefit: the premiums must be paid. Beveridge (para.21) was clear that the contributory principle was the right one: "benefit in return for contributions, rather than free allowances from the State, is what the people of Britain desire." This would strengthen the claim to benefit free of any means test, and further "insured persons should not feel that income for idleness, however caused, can come from a bottomless purse" (para.22). Then in 1954 the Phillips Committee on Provision for Old Age defended the contributory principle as "a valuable measure of social discipline" (Phillips, para.167). It may be useful when introducing a comprehensive system, free of means tests, to invoke such analogies, but clearly a scheme could be free both of means tests and contribution tests. It is clear also that there is barely any actuarial connection between contributions and benefits received. The scheme is financed on a pay-as-you-go basis, current contributions going to pay what the community decides current beneficiaries ought to receive. Future benefits are determined not by levels of past contributions but by what the community at the time considers right. It is this — the emphasis on adequacy of benefits rather than equity between contributors — that distinguishes social insurance from private insurance. For this also lies behind the absence of any weighting of contributions according to risk. Yet somehow the insurance principle clings on to bolster the idea that benefits must be based on contribution records, rather than need, and also to justify other eligibility provisions. Possibly the change of terminology in the 1973 Act, which no longer talks of National Insurance benefits, but of Social Security, means that a more realistic view of the system will be taken.

Perhaps a better justification for a contribution test is that the individual must demonstrate his attachment to the labour force by a certain amount of work. "It is the difficult task of the requirements for insured status to distinguish between (a) those who have worked long enough and recently enough in covered work to create a presumption that they have a substantial and continuing attachment to the labor force and (b) those who cannot be presumed to have such an attachment. In other words, where to draw the line depends on two elements: extent of attachment and recency of attachment" (U.S. Dept. of Labor). The British contribution test contains both these elements, although it is exceptionally complicated: a quagmire of contributions, credits, and (after 1975) earnings factors.

Contributions under the Social Security Act will not affect benefits before January 2, 1977, so that for some time the old contributions test will be important. This is set out in paragraph 1 of Schedule 2 to the National Insurance Act 1965. The claimant must have actually paid at least 26 contributions as an employed person, and to receive full benefit have either paid or had credited at least 50 such contributions in the relevant contribution year.

Old contribution years ran from the first complete week in March, June, September or December, depending on the letter at the end of the individual's National Insurance number.

Contributions in a year governed benefits in the year starting five months after the end of the contribution year. Thus if an individual's contribution year ran from March to March, those contributions would govern benefits from the next November. Under the 1975 Act everyone's contribution year is from April 6 to April 5 and the benefit year runs from January to January (Sched. 3, para.1(4) and s.13(7)). Special provisions have been made to achieve the transition, with some benefit years extended, some shortened, to end on January 1, 1977. Some contribution years have also been shortened, to end on April 5, 1975. In these cases contributions are specially credited to make up the missing weeks.

The 1975 Act retains a similar test, but some changes are necessitated by the move to earnings related contributions and the abolition of National Insurance cards and stamps. Class 1 contributions (*i.e.* for an employed earner) over the year give rise to an earnings factor, to be derived precisely from Tables, but to approximate to the minimum actual earnings sufficient to yield that amount of contributions (s.13(5)). The earnings factor is thus roughly the annual amount of earnings on which contributions have to be paid. The contribution test is then translated into (1) actually paying Class 1 contributions in one year giving an earnings factor of at least 25 times the lower earnings limit and (2) paying or being credited with Class 1 contributions in the relevant contribution year giving an earnings factor of at least 50 times the lower earnings limit. This appears to loosen the test considerably, especially for the higher paid. Contributions on earnings near the upper limit will give an earnings factor of several times the lower limit. Taking the figures for 1975-76, earnings of £69 per week for eight weeks will satisfy the second condition. It seems remarkably unfair to make the number of weeks' work necessary for qualification vary directly with the level of earnings. Nor is this necessitated by the change to earnings related contributions, for the test could have been put simply in terms of weeks worked during which there was liability for Class 1 contributions.

Contributions can be credited in a number of circumstances,

set out in the Social Security (Credits) Regulations 1975. Entitlement to unemployment or sickness benefit (independent of contribution conditions) carries with it entitlement to a credit (reg.9). Other provisions allow those just entering employment to build up entitlement quickly. Credited contributions are only relevant to entitlement to the basic flat-rate benefit, not to earnings-related supplement. It should be noted that up till April 1975 the conditions for credits were more stringent, requiring some record of contributions, but there were provisions for counting other classes of contributions as employed persons' contributions if at least 39 of the latter had actually been paid in the relevant contribution year. These rules apply to benefits up to the end of 1976.

Partial failure to satisfy the second contribution condition means only that benefit is paid at a reduced rate. The old law provides a sliding scale, but from 1977 there are only two alternatives. If the claimant's earnings factor is at least 37½ times the lower limit he gets 75 per cent.; if it is at least 25 times he gets 50 per cent. (Social Security (Unemployment, Sickness and Invalidity Benefit) Regulations 1975, reg.14). Increases for children are paid in full.

The contribution test has never required more than a relatively short period of actual employment, nor need this have been particularly recent. Relaxation of the rules on credits will allow more remote attachment to count. The earnings factor will allow a shorter period of attachment to count. Indefinite entitlement is ruled out because benefit can only be paid for 312 days without requalification by 13 weeks' work, but the test is fairly slack. This makes the continuance of the contributory principle harder to justify, when other methods exist for testing present attachment to the labour market. When there is a gap of nine months between contribution year and benefit year the relevance of that past period to current entitlement is slim.

Supplementary Benefit

Coverage here could scarcely be more general. By section 4(1) of the Supplementary Benefit Act 1966 every person in Great Britain aged 16 or over is entitled to benefit if his resources are insufficient to meet his requirements. Of course this declaration is hedged about with restrictions, but entitlement is based not on contributions, not even on citizenship, but simply on presence and need. The entire cost comes from general taxation.

Chapter 3

DISMISSAL AND UNEMPLOYMENT

Here I am concerned with the most basic eligibility conditions, the main question being whether the employment relation has to be severed in any particular way. By contrast, the more extensive and flexible conditions of the unemployment benefit scheme are considered. The comparison of the treatment of the reason for leaving employment is dealt with in the following chapter.

Wrongful Dismissal

The general law on the termination of contracts is beset by technicalities and conceptual distinctions. Contracts of employment add some special difficulties of their own to these overall problems. Since this is not an essay on the contract of employment as such, I shall try to limit the discussion to what is strictly relevant. However, it will be seen that these issues are important for unfair dismissal and redundancy and therefore some tentative explanations must be made.

Contracts of employment are commonly entered for an indefinite period and may be ended by either party at any time by giving notice of proper length. Termination on shorter notice is wrongful, in the absence of misconduct. The contract may provide what length of notice is to be given. In the absence of an express term one may be implied by the custom of the trade, providing the usual requirements for such implication can be proved. Otherwise, at common law reasonable notice must be given. What is reasonable depends on all the circumstances of the case, which go to a general assessment of the status of the particular employee. A Canadian judge, quoted in Hepple and O'Higgins, p.127, caught the flavour of the test well: "The question, what is reasonable notice, depends upon the capacity in which the employee is engaged, the general standing in the community of the class of persons, having regard to their profession, to which the employee belongs, the probable facility or difficulty the employee would have in procuring other employment in the case of dismissal, having regard to the demand for persons of that profession, and the general character of the services which the engagement contemplates" (Berk J. in *Speakman* v. *Calgary City* [1908] 9 W.L.R. 264 at p.265). To this list should be added length of service, so that there is no tariff for each job, for reasonableness will vary according to the particular employee. These subjective factors were mentioned in the recent decision of *Hill* v. *C.A. Parsons & Co. Ltd.* [1972] Ch. 305, where the period for a 63-year-old engineer with 35 years' service was set at at least six months.

Since 1963 statute has laid down minimum lengths of notice which neither contract nor custom can erode. These, extended in 1971, are now contained in the Contracts of Employment Act 1972, which lays down for at least 13 weeks' continuous employment (defined in Sched.1), one week's notice; two to five years, two weeks; five to 10 years, four weeks; 10 to 15 years, six weeks; over 15 years, eight weeks (s.1(1)). The Employment Protection Act 1975 (Sched.16, Part II, paras.1 and 2) reduces the qualifying period to four weeks, and for employment over two years, changes the method of calculation to one week's notice for each year of service up to a maximum of 12. A curiosity is section 1(3) which provides that these minimum notices cannot be excluded by contractual provision, but the Act "shall not be taken to prevent either party from waiving his right to notice on any occasion." It seems therefore that an employee may waive his right to notice on dismissal (presumably any earlier waiver would amount to a variation of the contract of employment and so be ineffective).

Termination of fixed term contracts before the expiry of the term is wrongful. If a contract may thus provide that it cannot be ended by notice, then presumably it may provide that notice can only be given in certain circumstances. The clerk in *McClelland* v. *Northern Ireland General Health Services Board* [1957] 1 W.L.R. 594 whose contract provided for dismissal only for a number of specified reasons and who was dismissed for a different reason (redundancy) was held by the House of Lords to have been wrongfully dismissed. Similarly, if the contract specifies a dismissal procedure, a dismissal that does not follow that procedure is a breach of contract. It may be that any hearing provided for must be carried out according to the principles of natural justice, although this has not yet been required in cases other than those involving union membership (*Taylor* v. *National Union of Seamen* [1967] 1 W.L.R. 532), office-holders (*Ridge* v. *Baldwin* [1964] A.C. 40), or where a statute regulates appointment and dismissal (see *e.g. Malloch* v. *Aberdeen Corporation* [1971] 1 W.L.R. 1578).

These rules regulate the ordinary termination by notice, but the employee is also entitled to damages if the employer repudiates the contract in some way. Attempts by the employer unilaterally to vary the terms of the contract, such as reducing agreed wages or requiring the employee to do work outside his contractual obligations or the area defined by the contract, are taken as an indication of an intention no longer to be bound by the contract. Work outside the contract includes exposure to physical risks outside the agreed duties, illegal acts, different kinds of work from those laid down in the contract, or, possibly, work required by unreasonable orders. This last category is not well-developed but support for it comes from the decision of the Court of Appeal in *Donovan* v. *Invicta Airlines Ltd.* [1970] Lloyd's Rep. 486. The plaintiff was a very experienced pilot, employed for a 17-week period. On three occasions his employers told him to fly aircraft which had mechanical failures and in unsafe weather conditions. Finally, after an unjustified reprimand, he left and succeeded in his action for damages covering the remainder of the 17 weeks. The ground was not so much the physical risks that he was exposed to, but that the employer's conduct was such as to make continuance of employment impossible for any self-respecting (*per* Fenton Atkinson L.J.) or reasonable (*per* Phillimore L.J.) pilot. This seems to amount to implying a term into the contract that only reasonable conduct would be required.

For the purposes of deciding if damages are payable there is no need to go further and decide exactly when and how the contract comes to an end. However, since these matters are crucial in considering unfair dismissal and redundancy I must make at least a tentative attempt to explain the common law situation. The point has arisen where some remedy other than damages is claimed. At one time it was considered trite law that a wrongful dismissal terminated the contract immediately. Although it was wrongful, the employee had no option but to leave. This rule was contrasted to the ordinary contract rule that a repudiation does not terminate the contract until it is accepted by the innocent party, who can elect either to affirm the contract or to treat it as at an end (see Lord Simon in *Heyman* v. *Darwins Ltd.* [1942] A.C. 356 at p.361). The contrast may not be so sharp if one accepts the refinement in *Harbutt's Plasticine Ltd.* v. *Wayne Tank and Pump Co. Ltd.* [1970] 1 Q.B. 447 that a breach may be so fundamental as to remove the innocent party's option and bring the contract to an end immediately, just like a frustrating event. The employment situation could be looked upon as one where a repudiatory (or fundamental) breach by the employer so destroyed the basis of the contract as to end it immediately.

A series of cases seems to be groping towards this position, although progress is far from straightforward. First, it was held in *Denmark Productions Ltd.* v. *Boscobel Productions Ltd.* [1969] 1 Q.B.699 that the true effect of a wrongful dismissal is to convert the claimant's right to wages into a right to damages. The authority for this rule was somewhat shaky (Freedland, p.316), but it was re-affirmed by Salmon and Sachs L.JJ. in the odd case of *Decro-Wall International S.A.* v. *Practitioners in Marketing Ltd.* [1971] 1 W.L.R. 361 on the ground that the claimant is not entitled to wages since he has not earned any by working. Thus in *Denmark* v. *Boscobel* the company dismissed from management of "The Kinks" could not claim their 10 per cent. share of remuneration under the contract or an account, but had to rely on damages. The result is that the claimant comes under the duty to mitigate his damages. He must take reasonable steps to find another suitable job. It does him no good to keep the contract alive, for if he attempts to "sit in the sun" collecting his wages he in fact destroys his right to damages. This explains why normally the claimant accepts the repudiation by leaving. "I doubt whether a wrongful dismissal brings a contract of service to an end in law, although no doubt in practice it does" (Salmon L.J. in *Decro-Wall*; at pp.369-370). Sachs L.J., "as at present advised," thought wrongful dismissal "a prime example of the type of case where an innocent party in practice must accept the repudiation" (*ibid.* at p.376). It must be emphasised that these statements are completely *obiter*, for the *Decro-Wall* case was about the sale of tiles and the attempted analogy to contracts of employment was, not surprisingly, rejected.

Nevertheless, they have been relied on for the decision in *Hill* v. *C.A. Parsons* (*supra*). Here the issue of continuance of the contract was raised because the Court of Appeal departed from the rule that the courts would not specifically enforce a contract of employment. The company gave Hill too short notice to terminate his contract, following a dispute about union membership. Hill applied for an injunction to prevent the company from acting on the notice. The Court of Appeal granted the injunction, holding first that in exceptional cases the court would grant a declaration that the contract of employment is still in existence, (relying on a statement to that effect by Lord Morris of Borth-y-Gest in *Francis* v. *Municipal Councillors of Kuala Lumpur* [1962] 1 W.L.R. 1411 at pp.1417-1418 (P.C.)). The exceptional circumstances seemed to be that by the time proper notice had expired the unfair dismissal provisions of the Industrial Relations Act 1971 would have been in force. On the question of whether the contract survived, Sachs L.J. was content to rely on his view in *Decro-Wall* and agree with Lord Denning M.R., whose argument is somewhat confusing. He says that short notice is not effective in law to terminate the contract. The employee can point this out to the employer and the notice can be withdrawn by agreement. But if the employer insists on terminating the contract on short notice then the consequence is that *"in the ordinary course of things*, the relationship of master and servant thereupon comes to end; for it is inconsistent with the confidential nature of the relationship that it should continue contrary to the will of one of the parties thereto" ([1972] Ch.314). This sounds like the old rule of law, giving the employee no option. But the rule is not inflexible. In proper cases, Lord Denning continues, the court will intervene and declare that the contract still exists. One senses another horrific voidability argument: insistence on the notice is effective to end the contract, unless the court decides that there are special circumstances. This particular position seems totally undesirable. The previous discussion was on the basis that either the contract continued if affirmed or ended if the repudiation was accepted, not that it ends, subject to resuscitation. The parties, particularly in the employment context, ought to know where they stand.

At this point the law was in a considerable mess. Courts concerned with redundancy and unfair dismissal have in general been able to cut through these problems, as will be seen below. However, the NIRC attempted some clarification in *Sanders* v. *Ernest A. Neale Ltd.* [1974] I.C.R. 565, where the *Hill* v. *Parsons* exception was said to be unusual, if not unique. Having disposed of some statements relied on in *Hill* v. *Parsons*, the court struck at the weak point of the *Decro-Wall* argument, that the employee cannot claim wages if he has not actually worked. It holds that if the employer prevents him from working he is still liable for wages. Since the dismissed man is agreed not to be entitled to wages, this must be because employment contracts are an exception to the general repudiation rule. However, *Hill* v. *Parsons* has to be accommodated, so is strictly limited to the situation where mutual confidence continues to exist. This was so in that case, where the employer was dismissing only in reaction to industrial pressure. Certainly, I would argue that mutual confidence can never exist when the employer's repudiation consists of a unilateral attempt to vary the terms of the contract. Most of the common law cases talk in terms of dismissal by notice: they should be limited to that situation. Where it is the employer's conduct which is repudiatory, all the authority points to the view that there can be no going back to the old contract. Take the seminal case of *Marriott* v. *Oxford Co-op* [1970] 1 Q.B. 186. Here the Co-op, after a dispute about down-grading Marriott, told him that he would be paid £1 a week less in a new job, starting a week later. Marriott protested but did the new job for three or four weeks until he left and claimed a redundancy payment. For these purposes it had to be decided if Marriott had been dismissed by the Co-op or whether he had consented to the change. The

Court of Appeal decided that the new terms were dictated and that Mariott could not be taken to have agreed to them by staying on under protest. The one possibility that no one suggested was that Marriott had kept the old contract alive by his protests: it was assumed that that contract had been terminated and the only issue was whether Marriott had agreed to its end. This is the approach which has been followed in the cases on redundancy and unfair dismissal. It is not entirely clear how far any of them rest on the words of the statute rather than the common law, but they clearly imply that if the employer does attempt unilaterally (rather than consensually) to vary the contract, that repudiation ends the contract forthwith. The contract is destroyed even more conclusively than if the employer insists on wrongful notice.

Finally, independent contractors are presumably subject only to the ordinary contract rules.

Unfair Dismissal

The basic condition for eligibility is that the employee has been dismissed. The Industrial Relations Act provided that an employee was dismissed in only two circumstances. These were if —

> "(a) the contract under which he is employed by the employer is terminated by the employer, whether it is so terminated by notice or without notice, or
> (b) where under that contract he is employed for a fixed term, that fixed term expires without being renewed under the same contract" (s.23(2)).

There was a good deal of concern about the omission of the third category of dismissal contained in the Redundancy Payments Act, which then covered termination by the employee without notice where the employer's conduct entitles the employee to do so. Fortunately, any possible scope for abuse and unfairness was circumvented by the NIRC. It built on the common law doctrine discussed above, and on decisions interpreting the definition of dismissal in the redundancy scheme discussed below. In a series of decisions, notably *Sutcliffe* v. *Hawker Siddeley Aviation Ltd.* [1973] I.C.R. 560, the NIRC held that repudiatory conduct by the employer terminated the contract for the purposes of section 23(2) providing that there was not real agreement to new terms by the claimant. The Trade Union and Labour Relations Act (Sched.1, para.5) includes the third category, without the requirement of no notice, so there is not now the same pressure to get cases within category (*a*).

However, some problems remain. One is where the claimant is given notice and then for some reason stops working before the expiry of the notice. In early cases there was a tendency to find that agreements to go early amounted to a consensual termination, so that the claimant was not dismissed. But the Court of Appeal in *Lees* v. *Arthur Greaves* (*Lees*) *Ltd.* [1974] I.C.R. 501 emphasised that such an agreement should only be found if there was real agreement with full knowledge of its implications. The alternative of an agreement that the claimant was not required to work out the rest of his notice was preferred in that case. The court approved the reluctance of the NIRC in *McAlwane* v. *Boughton Estates Ltd.* [1973] I.C.R. 470 to find a consensual termination in such circumstances. However, the line taken in that case, that a request to go a week early was a request to vary the date of the notice, should probably not be taken. Rather, the request should now be interpreted as one not to work out the remainder of the notice. It is right that there should be a fair amount of flexibility here, when it is seen that the Act specifically provides for notice by an employee already under notice from his employer still to count as dismissal by the employer (para. 23(3)). It would be unfortunate if the claimant were prejudiced by not giving notice.

Redundancy Payments

The Redundancy Payments Act 1965, s. 3(2) as substituted by Schedule 16, Part I, para 3. to the Employment Protection Act 1975, defines dismissal exhaustively as either (*a*) termination by the employer, (*b*) expiry of a fixed term, or (*c*) termination by the employee "with or without notice in circumstances (not falling within section 10(4) of this Act) such that he is entitled to terminate it without notice by reason of the employer's conduct." Section 10(4) deals with lock-outs. The definition is extended by section 22(1) under which termination of the contract by operation of law is in certain circumstances treated as termination by the employer. The main occasions are the death of a personal employer, dissolution of a partnership and receivership or winding-up of a company. Frustration also counts, but only if it is on account of an act by or affecting the employer.

In early cases, the courts tended to take a very strict view of this definition, emphasising its exhaustive quality. In *Morton Sundour Fabrics Ltd.* v. *Shaw* [1967] I.T.R. 84, a claimant given warning that he would be made redundant and put in touch with another employer, gave notice and left. The Divisional Court refused his claim for a redundancy payment since he had terminated the contract himself. The employer's warning was not notice, for that must operate on a particular date and "specify that date, or at least contain facts from which that date is ascertainable" (at p.86, *per* Diplock L.J.). The court felt bound to apply the strict words of the statute while appreciating the compelling reasons for a worker to find another job as soon as possible. The decision strikes at all the purposes of the Act. If the claimant has been deprived of a job by redundancy his hardship is the same no matter how the relationship was ended and it hardly encourages labour mobility or the efficient use of labour to make him hang on until dismissed to qualify for a payment. Moreover, it goes contrary to the government's recommended redundancy policy, now contained in the Code of Industrial Relations Practice, paras. 40-46, which stresses warnings as far in advance as possible and help in finding other jobs. The Code recommends schemes for voluntary redundancies. Employers can always ensure that a payment is made by themselves carrying out the formal act of dismissal, at the employee's request. Griffiths J. in *Burton, Allton & Johnson Ltd.* v. *Peck* [1975] I.R.L.R. 87 has recently confirmed that volunteering for redundancy does not necessarily mean a consensual termination rather than a dismissal under paragraph (*a*).

More recently the courts appear to have taken a more flexible view of the section and are prepared to mould it to fit better the needs of the Act. They have emphasised that they are not constrained by the technicalities of the common law, but try to look at realities. Thus paragraph (*c*) has become virtually redundant itself. The start is *Marriott's* case (*supra*). All three judges in the Court of Appeal were agreed that the Co-op's letter terminated the contract, but each put it differently. Lord Denning M.R. said that the letter evinced an intention no longer to be bound by the contract and was a repudiation. Cross L.J. emphasised that in reality the contract was terminated by the Co-op. Both these statements seem to leave no scope for paragraph (*c*): any conduct entitling the claimant to terminate will already have terminated the contract. So also does some of Winn L.J.'s judgment, where he says that if the contract is brought to an end either by notice from or conduct of the employer then there is a right to a payment. However, he also seemed to think there was a need for paragraph (*c*), although it is not clear what for.

Following *Marriott* judicial opinion was rather inconsistent, particularly within the Court of Appeal in *Duckworth* v. *P.F. Farnish & Co. Ltd.* [1970] I.T.R. 17. However, once the NIRC took over appeals in redundancy cases a more settled line appeared, linked to the common law authorities. One of the first cases was *GKN (Cwmbran) Ltd.* v. *Lloyd* [1972] I.C.R. 214, where it was held that the demotion of a skilled worker to an unskilled job at lower pay amounted to a termination under paragraph (*a*), relying on *Hill* v. *Parsons* [1972] Ch. 305. Thus four weeks' work in the new job was irrelevant. Any remaining doubts were removed by *Shields Furniture Ltd.* v. *Goff* [1973] I.C.R. 187 and *Sheet Metal Components Ltd.* v. *Plumridge* [1974] I.C.R. 373. Thus the NIRC was clear that for both redundancy and unfair dismissal purposes repudiatory conduct by the employer of itself terminated the contract, the only question being whether the employee agreed to the new terms.

The effect of these cases is codified in the new section 3(3)-(8) of the Redundancy Payments Act, under which, if the employer offers new employment to take effect within four weeks, and there are any differences in terms and conditions, there is a trial period. This is of four weeks, or longer by prior written agreement. The effect is that if the employee terminates the contract for any reason within the period, or if the employer terminates it for a reason connected with the change, the employee is treated as dismissed for the reason the original employment was ended. Now the parties should know exactly where they stand: an improvement on the judicial rule.

The Redundancy Payments Act contains complex provisions to deal with lay-offs and short-time working that are designed to prevent employers avoiding their liabilities. Where a redundancy situation exists some kind of work-sharing may be preferred by workers to straight dismissals, but employers must not be allowed to exploit this unfairly. Much depends on the precise form the lay-off, etc. takes. If the contract is terminated, with the hope of re-engagement, the employee can claim a payment if he likes. If he does not claim, the break will not break continuity if it can be described as temporary. If the lay-off takes the form of suspension, then unless there is an express or implied term in the contract authorising it, that is a repudiation by the employer, entitling the employee to a payment. Similarly, short-time working may be a breach of contract if reduced wages are the result. The special provisions are thus necessary in a fairly narrow range of situations. An employee is laid off when "an employee is employed under a contract on such terms and conditions that his remuneration thereunder depends on his being provided by the employer with work of the kind which he is employed to do, he shall ... be taken to be laid off for any week in respect of which, by reason that the employer does not provide such work for him, he is not entitled to any remuneration under the contract" (s.5(1)). Interpretation of the section is far from easy. The Industrial Tribunal (IT) in *Jones* v. *Harry Sherman Ltd.* [1969] I.T.R. 63 took the literal view that the section applies only to the same class of employees who in general are not entitled to wages if no work is available, but it may be wider. Short-time working is a situation in which diminution of work causes the worker's remuneration for any week to be less than half a week's pay (s.5(2)). This is quite a restrictive definition since overtime which is not obligatory on both parties is excluded from pay under the Employment Protection Act, Sched. 4.

After four consecutive weeks of lay-off or short-time (LOST) or six weeks out of 13 the claimant may serve a notice of intention to claim a redundancy payment. If the employer does not object then the claimant has to give notice within four weeks to terminate the contract to be entitled to a payment. If the employer objects the issue goes to an IT which decides if it was reasonably to be expected that the claimant would within four weeks of the first notice enter on a period of employment of at least 13 weeks without further LOST. If it was, then there is no entitlement. If not the claimant gets the payment by giving notice. Employment means under the existing contract (*Neepsend Steel and Tool Corp. Ltd.* v. *Vaughan* [1972] I.C.R. 278), so that the employer cannot escape by offering other work. The main drawback of this process is the length of time it may take for the issues to be resolved, and its procedural pitfalls. Finally there is the all-embracing nature of section 7(3) which provides that no account shall be taken of weeks of LOST "wholly or mainly attributable to a strike or lock-out, whether the strike or lock-out is in the trade or industry in which the employee is employed or not and whether it is in Great Britain or elsewhere."

Unemployment Benefit

Put at its simplest, benefit is payable for each day of unemployment, but this needs considerable expansion. First, benefit is not paid for isolated days. A day must be part of a period of interruption of employment, which means two days of unemployment in a six day period (National Insurance Act 1965, s.20(1)(*d*), Social Security Act 1975, s.17(1)(*d*)). Any such periods not separated by more than 13 weeks are added together to form one period of interruption. Nor is benefit paid at all for the first three days of any period of interruption (1965 Act, s.19(6), 1975 Act, s.14(3)). Secondly, if a claimant has received benefit for 312 days, he is not entitled again until he has requalified, which means working for at least 21 hours a week for 13 weeks (1975 Act, s.18).

The more difficult question is the meaning of unemployment. Under the National Insurance (Unemployment and Sickness Benefit) Regulations 1967 the claimant has to show that he is unemployed and available for employment (reg.7(1)(*a*)). This provision is omitted from the regulations governing claims after January 1, 1977, but presumably the only change is to the onus of proof, for the 1975 Act talks of a day of unemployment (s.14(1)(*a*)) and the need for the claimant to be available for employment (s.17(1)(*a*)). These are important issues, first because if the claimant fails he is completely ineligible for benefit while the conditions last. There is no question of disqualification for a limited period. Further, they are in some ways at the heart of the system. As Haber and Murray point out in relation to the United States, the "application of the test of eligibility and availability for work has an important bearing on the successful operation of the unemployment insurance program. If the tests are applied loosely or ineffectively so that a substantial number of people draw benefits who are not genuinely in the labor market, it will throw the system into disrepute. On the other hand, if these tests are applied mechanically, inflexibly and without treating the claimant as a human being, one of the chief values of unemployment insurance, the preservation of the self-respect of the unemployed worker, will be lost" (Haber and Murray, p.265).

The issues of unemployment and availability tend to merge into one another, but it is possible to deal with them separately.

(1) The word "unemployment" is defined nowhere, but the principle is, according to R(U) 3/67, that a person is employed if he is gainfully occupied in employment and unemployed if he is not so gainfully occupied. Employment includes "any trade, business, profession, office or vocation" (1965 Act, s.114(1), 1975 Act, Sched. 20), and by implication employment under a contract of service. The result is that prima facie anyone so occupied is not unemployed. However, there is help in regulation 7(1)(*i*) of the 1967 Regulations, which provides that a day shall not be treated as a day of unemployment "if on that day an insured person is following any occupation (…) unless the earnings derived from that occupation, in respect of that day, do not exceed 75 pence …, and unless he is available on that day for full-time employment in some employed contributor's employment and the occupation which he is following is consistent with that

full-time employment and, if he is following that occupation under a contract of service, it is not his usual main occupation; ..." The equivalent provision under the 1975 Act (reg.7(1)(*h*) of the Social Security (Unemployment, Sickness and Invalidity Benefit) Regulations 1975) applies to a person engaged in any employment, so that the point of the following decisions will be removed. The 1967 regulation appears to extend non-eligibility to the following of any occupation, but the Commissioners restrict this to gainful occupations (R(U) 2/67, para.5). The point was elaborated in C.U. 25/72, concerning two members of the Newton Abbot Claimants Union. They did work in return for a donation in one case to the Union, and in the other, an independent charity. Neither occupation was gainful, for the claimants had no expectation of personal gain or benefit. But the Commissioner warned against other ingenious attempts to evade the regulations.

This principle has enabled the Commissioners to distinguish between various kinds of training course. Thus in R(U) 2/67 a claimant who was paid small sums for therapeutic work at a centre for the mentally disordered was held not to be following an occupation. This was in contrast to R(U) 4/64, where a worker in a local authority sheltered factory was disentitled. Similarly, R(U) 3/67 departed from the previously accepted rule in holding that a claimant on a firm's selection and training course, receiving only expenses, was merely qualifying for employment, and so unemployed. Since the case was based on the general definition of unemployment it is possible that some trainees might be said to be following an occupation. It is fortunate that such a possibility is removed under the 1975 Regulations.

A particular problem is where a claimant receives wages under a contract of service, although does not actually work. Here the claimant is taken to be occupied in employment. Thus the well-known "disappointment money" case (R(U)

11/64) is quite in line with other decisions. The claimant dock worker was allocated to a ship which did not arrive on time. In accordance with an implied term in his contract he was paid £1 (less 10/7d stamp!) and was held not to be unemployed for that day although he was free for any other work. The trouble is that the authorities will not divide up a day into parts. Although his contract ended at about 12.30 a.m. when the payment was made, he was employed for part of the day and that is enough. The point is emphasised by R(U) 4/71, where a claimant received holiday pay for the New Year running from noon on December 31 to noon on January 3. Though he only got three days' pay he was held not to be unemployed on all four days. Thus it does not matter that only a small proportion of wages are paid, nor can a claimant escape under regulation 7(1)(*i*) if he is engaged in his usual main occupation. The only escape is if the money is not paid under the contract. The student hostel cleaner in R(U) 6/68 who was paid £4 retaining fee on returning after being laid off for the summer succeeded on this ground. It was not in return for any services rendered, even being available to work if necessary. A similar approach is taken to claimants receiving payments under guaranteed week agreements, though not required to work. They are not unemployed if their contract expressly or impliedly obliges them to place their services at the employer's disposal (R(U) 10/73, 11/73). In contrast, a claimant who worked under contract but received no wages was not unemployed. (R(U) 5/75).

There is recognition of the hardship caused by a rigid application of the unemployment test in regulation 7(1)(*i*) (reg.7(1)(*h*) of the 1975 Regulations), but the relief it offers is rather limited. First the earnings limit for the day is very low. If the earnings cover employment for a longer period than a day then they are averaged out. It is sometimes a difficult question to decide over what period to spread earnings. In several cases professional footballers who play once a week but are paid a weekly wage have been held to earn that over the week, not just on one day (see most recently R(U) 10/72 and discussion in R(U) 1/73 and 4/74). The claimant must be available for employment (the meaning of this is discussed below), and the occupation must be consistent with full-time employment. The difference between these two requirements has been the source of some puzzlement. It was pointed out in R(U) 4/64 that it is the occupation that has to be looked at, not the claimant's intentions. Clearly if the hours of work cannot be re-arranged and destroy the prospects of full-time work (like the park-keeper working from 4 p.m. in R(U) 12/59) the occupation is inconsistent. But if the hours can be re-arranged, the rule laid down in R(U) 4/64 and 2/67 was that if they can be re-arranged without reduction in number so that the occupation can be carried on together with full-time employment then it is consistent. However, in C.U. 9/69 the requirement that the hours worked should not be reduced was dropped. The occupation there was as part-proprietor of a shop, which could be abandoned at any time for another job. When the claimant is filling his spare time like this, and can satisfy the earnings and availability tests, it seems fair to allow him to claim. Indeed the other rule would seem to discourage part-time work to preserve job skills and combat the demoralisation and lassitude brought on by unemployment. The new rule has been followed in C.U. 21/72 and 1/73, and does not seem to have deprived the consistency test of its meaning as was feared. Finally, the occupation must not be the usual main occupation. It is often said that it must be subsidiary, but presumably the claimant without any usual occupation is not caught. The issue here is largely one of fact.

(2) On the question of availability there is again a combination of case law developed by the Commissioners and regulations. To take the general principles first: "Ever since 1930 the definition of availability given by the Umpire in

Umpire's Decision 6986/30 has been accepted as authoritative: 'As a general rule applicants cannot be regarded as available for work unless they are prepared to accept at once any offers of suitable employment brought to their notice''' (R(U) 1/53). Thus the claimant must not be prevented by some other activity from accepting employment and also must not unduly restrict the kind of job he will take.

Regulation 7(1)(*i*) is usually invoked to deal with other occupations, but the general test is incorporated in it and is also relevant where what the claimant does is not a gainful occupation for the purposes of regulation 7(1)(*i*) or employment under regulation 7(1)(*h*) of the 1975 Regulations. The approach is exemplified in R(U) 34/53. The claimant was a local councillor, who had to leave home before 9 a.m. to attend meetings. He was held unavailable on those days since he was unable, during normal business hours, to receive and act upon a notification of an interview with an employer. Such rules could obviously be used to exert an undesirable amount of control over a claimant's life if interpreted strictly, but even if the authorities wanted to, they have neither time nor resources to do so. For instance, claimants in practice are required only to visit the employment exchange once a week, not every day. One situation in which there is intervention is where the claimant goes away on holiday. Here an elaborate test was laid down by the Umpire in Decision 7550/35. The claimant had to satisfy three conditions: (1) that he was ready and willing immediately to curtail his absence to accept at once any suitable employment, (2) that he had taken reasonable and satisfactory steps to ensure that any opportunity would be brought to his notice, and (3) nothing in the nature or location of his absence would prevent him from accepting suitable employment at once. This test has been accepted in a number of decisions (*e.g.* R(U) 3/65), but the trend of recent decisions has been away from its exclusive use to asking more broadly if the claimant is available for each day. In R(U) 4/66 it was said that the test was developed at a time of mass unemployment and that modern conditions might justify less leniency. In C.U. 3/67 it is pointed out that the test applied to periods of unemployment, whereas now availability must be decided day by day. This makes it more difficult for someone on holiday to be available: the claimant, who said he would return within 24 hours if a job came up, was held not to be available on any one day. It is not clear that this adds much to the Umpire's test, for the claimant would have been caught by condition (3). Similarly, the claimant in R(U) 4/66 failed to satisfy the last two conditions of the test, so that a claimant who satisfies the old test has not yet been held unavailable.

Thus a claimant has to be ready to accept a job at any time. But what kinds of jobs must he be prepared to accept? How far may he restrict himself to certain jobs? Here is a test of the claimant's present attachment to the labour market (see Freeman, p.124). In general the market is described in terms of the individual and the services he offers. He must be available for *suitable* work and the test is not if work is available, but if the claimant is.

Regulation (7)(1)(*b*) of the 1967 Regulations (reg.7(1)(*a*) of the 1975 Regulations) provides that —

"where in respect of any day a person places restrictions on the nature, hours, rate of remuneration or locality or other conditions of employment which he is prepared to accept and as a consequence of those restrictions has no reasonable prospects of securing employment, that day shall not be treated as a day of unemployment unless —

(i) he is prevented from having reasonable prospects of securing employment consistent with those restrictions only as a result of adverse industrial conditions in the locality or localities concerned which may reasonably be regarded as temporary, and, having

regard to all the circumstances, personal and other,
the restrictions which he imposes are reasonable; or

(ii) the restrictions are nevertheless reasonable in view
of his physical condition; or

(iii) the restrictions are nevertheless reasonable having
regard both to the nature of his usual occupation
and also to the length of time which has elapsed
since he became unemployed.''

The claimant must impose restrictions for the regulations
to operate, and as a consequence have no reasonable
prospects of employment. The restrictions are usually
express, but in C.U. 5/74 it was argued that persistence in
wearing shoulder length hair was a restriction. The Commissioner, while not attracted by this, did not have to decide the
issue. If no prospects exist for the claimant because of
immutable characteristics, such as age, sex, race, physical
capabilities, he should still be held available for work. The
claimant is not wilfully unemployed and unemployment
resulting from the state of the labour market is exactly the
kind that most deserves compensation. This principle gained
belated recognition in C.U. 3/71. Although the claimant had
placed restrictions on his employment it was held that his
absence of prospects of employment arose not from those
restrictions, but from his age (64). It was notoriously difficult
for a man of 64 to get a job of the type the claimant was
capable of. A similar approach in the case of a married
woman was hinted at in R(U) 31/58, but I suspect that the
argument is not made as often as it should be. It is not clear
which factors are so attached to the claimant that they of
themselves deprive him of prospects. Presumably so far as a
physical condition goes it does not matter which view is taken
because of condition (ii). Further the regulation applies only
if there is some limitation as to the kind of job acceptable. If
the claimant is not prepared to work at all on a particular day

he is clearly not available, whatever the reason (R(U) 15/58). Whether prospects of employment are reasonable is largely a question of fact. No standard by which reasonableness is to be judged seems to have emerged from the Commissioners' decisions. In C.U. 3/74 it was said that regulation 7(1)(*b*) only came into play if the claimant's chances of employment were virtually nil, but most cases do not seem to take this narrow line. The claimant's past record of employment subject to similar restrictions is relevant, as is length of unemployment, but all turns on the particular facts. One particular situation that sometimes arises is a restriction to work for only a few days a week or for part-time work. If such work is not available then the claimant may be unavailable even on the days he is prepared to work, unless one of the conditions is satisfied.

These are fairly strictly construed. It is not good enough that the restrictions are reasonable in the claimant's personal circumstances. The husband in R(U) 6/59 was available only for afternoons since the family had decided that the wife was to be principal bread-winner and he had to look after the children in the mornings. He gained no assistance from the regulation. It was irrelevant that the restriction was demanded by the style of life he had adopted. Nor does it do any good for a wife to say that she has to look after her husband (R(U) 17/57). This seems harsh for claimants who are genuinely seeking work, for their unemployment is caused by labour market conditions as well as their own circumstances. However, a subjective test has proved unworkable in the past and it may be that some extension of the three conditions is the answer.

There is not much authority on the meaning of the first condition. "Industrial conditions" appears to mean general business conditions, so that an agreement between the two English film manufacturing firms not to employ the other's ex-employees did not count (C.U. 15/66). "Temporary" imports a degree of abnormality or unforeseeability. A recurrent seasonal fluctuation is not good enough, even though the conditions are of limited duration. Where the claimant lived in a seaside town where the prospects of employment fell off sharply outside the summer season, these conditions were not temporary. They were annually recurrent and their advent and duration were known and foreseeable (R(U) 3/59). The question of what restrictions are justified by physical conditions is one of fact, although not always straightforward. Perhaps the trickiest condition is (iii). According to R(U) 3/59 the rationale is to safeguard job skills by protecting a claimant who restricts himself from accepting employment different from or on less satisfactory conditions than his usual occupation. Thus the fact that the claimant there was only available in the winter because she worked in the summer as a domestic helper in her mother's boarding house was said to follow from purely personal reasons and have nothing to do with the nature of the occupation of domestic helper. Similarly, the actor who restricted his availability to certain days when he was not needed by the BBC did not do so by reason of his occupation, but because of his particular commitments to the BBC (R(U) 1/69). Clearly in neither of these cases was any question of preserving job skills involved, but one must go to the regulation, not its gloss. Everything depends on how widely one chooses to define "occupation." Obviously personal factors enter as the definition becomes narrower and more precise. So the occupation of the claimant in R(U) 3/59 could be defined as "summer domestic helper," but the Commissioner chose the more general description. Again, and more forcibly, the irrelevance of the reasonableness of the claimant's conduct in the abstract is underlined. Job skills cannot be protected for ever. The regulation makes this clear, but there is a lot of leeway in deciding how long a claimant can reasonably restrict himself to his usual occupation. The availability of employment at various grades in the locality must be considered, among other factors (C.U. 11/67). One important factor is the claimant's retirement from his usual job. Then he cannot be judged solely on "what was, but no longer is, the nature of his usual occupation" (C.U. 11/67). Often the claimant is given some time to lower his sights, but may be held unavailable immediately if he tries to maintain completely unrealistic standards. This was the fate of the retired technical manager of 62 who would only accept a job as a technical manager at at least £5,000 per annum close to his home (R(U) 6/72). If a claimant does satisfy one of the conditions, then he cannot be held to be unavailable on the general test because of the restrictions. It is true that regulation 7(1)(*b*) does not deem the claimant to be available, but the rule was established in R(U) 4/57 in order to save regulation 7(1)(*b*) from redundancy.

Thus it can be seen that the issue of availability leads to a number of rather detailed decisions, often turning on the insurance officer's opinion of the claimant's intentions and of the possibilities of the labour market. The recent survey of characteristics of the unemployed pointed out that although assessments of job prospects by local offices were generally sound, no clear-cut judgments could be made about individuals. Over 28 per cent. of those assessed as having poor prospects in June 1973 had been employed some time in the following six months (D.E. Gazette, March 1974, p.215). One may question the testing of claimants against hypothetical situations instead of concrete job offers. One claimant did argue that she could not be held unavailable until she had been offered at least one job, but this was rejected (R(U) 44/53). It might be ridiculous to have to go through the form of offering a job it is known the claimant will reject, but that would seem quite sensible in marginal cases. This is reinforced by criticisms by the Commissioners of the way in which statements of availability are obtained. The form used is UI 672, which asks, *inter alia*, what type of employment the claimant is prepared to accept and what minimum salary he requires. The answers are taken as expressing the restrictions the claimant places on employment. Some of the questions were criticised in C.U. 3/71 for talking of what is required rather than what he is prepared to accept. I do not know if the form has been changed since. Even so the questions are not clear, for many people would not realise that saying what they are prepared to accept is taken as a statement that they will not accept anything else.

There is evidence that the significance of their answers has not always been pointed out to claimants, a procedure strongly criticised in C.U. 14/67 as contrary to the fundamental principle of equity that a person should not be put to an election unless he understands his rights. The latest leaflet (NI 12) says that there will be a special interview if it is thought any restrictions may affect entitlement, and precise details obtained of what the claimant is prepared to accept. This procedure is obviously desirable.

Nevertheless, the broad structure of the rules may still be questioned. Altman, in his study of the American system, wrote "The role of the availability requirements (and the other eligibility conditions) in the unemployment compensation structure may be best conceived as a broad, rough test that the claimant must meet. It is a gross sieve designed to block the clearly unfit from entering and remaining in the benefit system .... Some claimants will get past such a preliminary examination despite their actual unwillingness and inability to work. They will not be numerous. For them there is a secondary line of defence to prevent them from penetrating too deeply, a finer sieve. That is the test of offered suitable work." (Altman, p.87) It seems to me that in Great Britain we try to sieve too finely too soon.

Finally, one should note section 20(1)(*b*) of the 1965 Act (1975 Act, s.17(1)(*b*)), which prevents claims for days on which the claimant does not normally work if his employment is suspended for less than a full week, and regulation 7(1)(*f*) of the 1967 Regulations (1975 Regulations, reg. 7(1)(*e*)) disentitling anyone who works to the full extent normal in a week. These needlessly complex provisions cannot be discussed here, but have recently been dealt with by Ogus.

Supplementary Benefit

The general right to benefit is cut into a number of eligibility conditions. First, persons engaged in remunerative full-time work are excluded (Supplementary Benefit Act 1966, s.8(1)), except for cases of urgency (s.13). According to the Supplementary Benefits Handbook, full-time means working the recognised week in the particular trade or employment (para.2). Thus part-time workers are included in the scheme. The condition does not apply to self-employed workers whose earning power is substantially reduced by disability (s.8(3)). By regulation (Supplementary Benefit (General) Regulations 1966, reg.2) those starting full-time work are not disentitled for a period of 15 days, though any money actually received from the employer in that period must be taken account of. This is to prevent hardship caused by the fact that wages do not usually start being paid until the end of the first or second week. Payments can be made to people returning to work after strikes, but the Social Security Act 1971 introduced an elaborate scheme for repayment of any benefit in these circumstances through deduction from pay. One doubts if the amounts saved will outweigh the additional administrative costs.

The Supplementary Benefits Commission (SBC) is given power by section 11 of the Act to make receipt of supplementary allowance subject to the condition of registration for employment. Thus the condition cannot be imposed on anyone over pension age, but is normally applied to anyone else who is capable of work. Lone parents with dependent children under 16 and blind people not accustomed to working outside the home are excluded (Handbook, para.8). The condition may be waived according to circumstance for a further three groups: (1) people required at home to care for sick relatives, (2) women widowed in later middle life with no experience of employment and some evidence of ill-health, (3) people on training or educational courses (para.9). Waiver is rare in this third category. People on Training Opportunities Scheme courses or other courses for the unemployed are likely to be eligible, but for ordinary students it is limited to those who fail to qualify for a hardship allowance because they are not married (para.163). They can of course claim during vacations subject to the normal registration requirement. There is a great deal more flexibility to react to personal circumstances than in the unemployment benefit system. The idea is to keep the claimant in touch with the labour market and give him the benefits of the job finding function of the employment service. In these cases benefit is paid by the Department of Employment.

There are additional powers for dealing with claimants who are reluctant to work, but these are better left to the chapter on Neglect of Job Opporunities. Similarly the question of when resources fall below requirements merges into that of calculating the amount of benefit and is dealt with in the chapter on Benefits.

Chapter 4

THE REASON FOR TERMINATION OF EMPLOYMENT

Here the concern is partly with the definitions of redundancy and unfair dismissal, which pick out certain categories of the unemployed for special treatment, and partly with the extent to which misconduct or voluntary leaving on the part of the claimant disqualifies him for benefit. Again it is interesting to see how far objectives other than compensation operate, and the role of the rules as a sanction behind industrial discipline and as a work incentive.

Wrongful Dismissal

Before damages can be awarded the contract must be broken by the employer, as discussed in Chapter 3. The employee who leaves voluntarily, not in response to the employer's repudiation, has no claim. What is important here is the question of when the employer is entitled to dismiss the claimant summarily, without giving the contractual notice. The principles are roughly the same as those governing the employer's conduct, in that it is conduct indicating a repudiation of contractual obligations which justifies dismissal. The suggestion put forward by the NIRC in *Hare* v. *Murphy Bros.* [1973] I.C.R. 331 that such conduct amounts to termination by the employee seems now to have been rejected. The Court of Appeal in that case [1974] I.C.R. 603) held that the sentence of a year in prison frustrated the contract. Even so this means the contract is ended, independently of any act by the employer. In *Forgings & Presswork Ltd.* v. *McDougall* [1974] I.C.R. 532 the principle was limited to where the employee has put it out of his power to perform the contract, which will not be the usual case. Nevertheless, there is still a degree of doubt, especially since the argument has not yet been made outside the unfair dismissal context.

There are quite a number of decisions on summary dismissal, but most are decisions of fact about whether the claimant's conduct justifies it. Since at base each decision depends on all the circumstances of the case, only rather vague guidelines can be put down. Breach of some duties is regarded as so serious as normally to justify dismissal. Taking secret profits, revealing trade secrets, dealing dishonestly with the employer's property would be examples. *Sinclair* v. *Neighbour* [1967] 2 Q.B. 279, where the bookmaker's clerk who borrowed £15 from his employer's till leaving an IOU was held to be rightfully dismissed, illustrates both this principle and the importance of all the circumstances. Bookmaker's employees must not be encouraged to bet with other people's money! It seems that any act of disobedience to a lawful order was once put in the same category. Thus in the notorious *Turner* v. *Mason* (1845) 14 M. & W.112 the court upheld the dismissal of a maid who, refused permission to visit her dying mother, left nonetheless. The moral duty did not affect the legal duty. The legal duty is only the contractual duty, so that decisions implying limitations to the employer's powers where the express contract is silent have softened the harshness. Also the courts now take a more flexible viewpoint and ask if the context of disobedience is such that it indicates a repudiation of the fundamental obligations of the contract. This trend was first marked in *Laws* v. *London Chronicle Ltd.* [1959] 1 W.L.R. 698 to protect a secretary who followed her immediate superior out of a room contrary to the orders of his boss after a row between the two men. It was confirmed in the colourful case of *Pepper* v. *Webb* [1969] 1 W.L.R. 514 in a slightly wider application. The claimant, a gardener, refused an order to do some planting just before he was due to leave work, saying "I couldn't care less about your bloody greenhouse or your sodding garden." He was summarily dismissed and the Court of Appeal rejected his claim. His outburst came after a history of unsatisfactory behaviour, and was regarded either as a wilful refusal to obey (Karminski L.J.) or as indicating repudiation of his obligations, which were precisely to care for the garden (Harman L.J.) However, too much importance should not be attached to mere swearing, even in a domestic context, as *Wilson* v. *Racher* [1974] I.C.R. 428 shows. The claimant, another gardener but hitherto well-behaved and competent, reacted to a series of trivial complaints with "obscene" language. The Court of Appeal did not regard his conduct on this isolated occasion as making the continuance of the relationship impossible. It seems that *Pepper* v. *Webb* shows that the trivial last straw may justify dismissal.

Conduct outside the course of employment may justify dismissal, but where this amounts only to harming the employer's interests rather than, say, disclosing trade secrets, fairly strong evidence is needed of its harm. The issue is predominantly one of fact, depending on the nature of the job and on the social attitudes of the day. The tests laid down in *Pearce* v. *Foster* (1886) 17 Q.B.D. 536 are so vague as to offer no assistance, *e.g.* conduct "so grossly immoral that all reasonable men would say that he cannot be trusted" (Lord Esher M.R.). The court upheld the dismissal of a clerk who had merely gambled heavily on the stock exchange with his own money, when his job involved advising on stocks and shares. Simple incompetence does not justify summary dismissal, unless the claimant has warranted his competence before being engaged. This at least is so if there is no express term of the contract about satisfactory performance. In

Diggle v. *Ogston Motor Co*. (1915) 84 L.J.K.B. 2165 where the claimant's employment was subject to the satisfaction of the directors, he was rightfully dismissed unless he could show that no reasonable board of directors could have been dissatisfied. The contract may provide specifically for dismissal in circumstancès that would not be serious enough at common law, although it is impossible to say how usual such clauses are. Wedderburn (p.108) reports that in a 1949 agreement BOAC acquired the right to dismiss anyone drinking intoxicating liquor or taking drugs to excess, and for conduct likely to be prejudicial to the interest of the employers. At least here the condition is expressed object-ively, so that its existence could be challenged, but the addition of subjective language, as in *Diggle* v. *Ogston*, means that challenge under the common law is only possible for dishonesty.

It is the existence of the reason justifying dismissal that matters, regardless of whether the employer relied on that reason for dismissal or even if he was ignorant of its existence. The rule, laid down in *Boston Deep Sea Fishing & Ice Co*. v. *Ansell* (1888) 39 Ch.D 339, has been doubted, but has been strongly re-asserted as correct in both law and common sense by the Court of Appeal in *Cyril Leonard & Co*. v. *Simo Securities Trust Ltd*. [1972] 1 W.L.R. 80. Nonetheless, here, as in other matters, the unfair dismissal legislation may lead to a different practical result. If the employer does not exercise his right to dismiss summarily when he does learn of misconduct it seems he cannot revive it later (*Phillips* v. *Foxall* (1872) L.R. 7 Q.B. 666 at p.680 *per* Blackburn J.). The misconduct can then only form part of the history.

Unfair Dismissal

It is for the employer to show what was the principal reason for dismissal (Trade Union and Labour Relations Act 1974,

Sched.1, para.6(1)(*a*)). In order to satisfy paragraph 6(1), the
reason must be either (a) related to the capability or
qualifications of the claimant for doing his job; (b) related to
the claimant's conduct; (c) that the claimant was redundant;
(d) that the claimant's continued employment is contrary to
some enactment (para.6(2)); or be some other substantial
reason of a kind such as to justify the dismissal of someone in
the claimant's position (para.6(1)(*a*)). Capability means
capability by reference to skill, aptitude, health or other
physical or mental quality and qualifications mean any
degree, diploma or other academic, technical or professional
qualification relevant to the claimant's position (para.6(9)).
Then, in general, the question of fairness depends on
whether, having regard to the reason shown by the employer,
he can satisfy the IT that in the circumstances (having regard
to equity and the substantial merits of the case) he acted
reasonably in treating it as a sufficient reason for dismissing
the claimant (para.6(8)).

There are a number of circumstances in which a dismissal is
deemed to be unfair or fair. First, the Employment
Protection Act 1975, s.34, deals with dismissal on grounds of
pregnancy. Dismissal for reasons connected with pregnancy is
unfair unless the woman is thereby incapable of adequately
doing her work or her continued employment would be
illegal. To escape under these exceptions the employer must
offer the woman any suitable alternative vacancy which
exists. Further, failure to permit a woman to return to work
after pregnancy in exercise of her rights under section 49 of
the Act counts as a dismissal for the reason for which return
was refused (s.50). By section 51 dismissal of a replacement
expressly hired until a pregnant woman returns is for a
substantial reason, etc., under paragraph 6(1)(*b*), although
the dismissal may still be unfair under paragraph 6(8).

However, more controversial is the situation where there is
a union membership agreement. A union membership

agreement is, by section 30(1) of the Trade Union and Labour Relations Act 1974 an agreement or arrangement between one or more independent trade unions and one or more employers or employers' associations relating to an identifiable class of employees which "has the effect in practice of requiring the employees for the time being of the class to which it relates (whether or not there is a condition to that effect in their contract of employment) to be or become a member of the union or one of the unions which is or are parties to the agreement or arrangement or of another specified independent trade union." Specified unions here include those recognised by the parties to the agreement as equivalent to unions specified in the agreement itself. If it is the practice under the agreement for employees of the same class as the claimant to join a specified union and the claimant is not or proposes not to be a member of a specified union, then a dismissal for that reason is deemed to be fair (para.6(5)). Here a union is treated as specified if (i) the Advisory Conciliation and Arbitration Service has made an operative recommendation for recognition covering the employee in question (it seems unnecessary for the recommendation to be for recognition of the *union* in question: an oversight?) or (ii) the union has a live recognition reference before the ACAS. However, if the claimant "genuinely objects on grounds of religious belief to being a member of any trade union whatsoever" such dismissal is deemed to be unfair (para. 6(5)). An IT will be bound to take account of the provisions of any charter of guidance on the freedom of the press produced under section 1A of the Trade Union and Labour Relations (Amendment) Act 1976, particularly those relating to the application of union membership agreements to journalists (s.1A(10)). Dismissal for joining or proposing to join an independent trade union or for taking or preparing to take part in its activities at any appropriate time (see para. 6(4A)) is unfair, as is dismissal for refusing to join a

non-independent union (para.6(4)). Reasons deemed unfair
are called inadmissible reasons. Finally, anyone selected for
redundancy when others are in the same situation is unfairly
dismissed if he was selected for an inadmissible reason or (in
the absence of special circumstances) in breach of a
customary arrangement or agreed procedure (para.6(7)).
There are also special provisions dealing with dismissal during
a lock-out or industrial action (para.7).

These complex provisions are the result of the notorious
Lever amendments in the 1974 Act, additions by the
Employment Protection Act and finally some simplification
by the Amendment Act in 1976. Some of the trickiest
problems of interpretation relating to union membership have
been removed. For instance, ITs no longer have to decide
what might be reasonable grounds for refusing to be a
member of a particular union, or whether the practice of
union membership is sufficiently universally enforced, *cf.*
the "Ferrybridge Six" case. The Press Charter provisions
appear to add little extra direction to ITs. Thus the issues that
remain are largely the formidable ones of principle, which
extend beyond the scope of this book. Of the remaining legal
problems, one may be the scope of the protection given when
the ACAS has made an operative recommendation for
recognition. Another may be if an employee alleges that his
purported expulsion from a union is void; here the IT may be
drawn into a prediction of the result of an action against the
union in the common law courts.

However, ITs will usually not be concerned with these
special problems. Although in most cases the legislation
leaves the definition of unfairness in the hands of the IT (in
contrast to ILO Recommendation No. 119 and the 1970
Labour Bill, which both set out a number of automatically
unfair reasons for dismissal), the courts have laid down some
legal guidelines. These guidelines are of varying strength. The
courts emphasise that providing the IT directs itself properly

on the law they will not interfere with the decision on the facts. For a recent statement of these principles, see *Moore* v. *Aluminium Platers (Leeds) Ltd.*]1976] I.C.R. 83.

The Act does not say what happens if the employer fails to show one of the reasons mentioned, but *Midland Foot Comfort Centre Ltd.* v. *Richmond* [1973] I.C.R. 219 confirms that the result is that the employer loses. This is of particular importance where the employer yields to threats of industrial action which by paragraph 15 and section 76(5) of the Employment Protection Act 1975, are to be ignored. The result is that the employer can show no reason for dismissal and therefore has to pay compensation, having now lost the right granted by the Industrial Relations Act to recover it from the third party applying the pressure. The reason to be looked at is not necessarily the one which immediately precipitates dismissal, but the reason as a matter of common sense, according to *Turner* v. *Wadham Stringer Commercials* [1974] I.C.R. 277. Reasons (a) — (d) have given few problems. *Blackman* v. *Post Office* [1974] I.C.R. 151 points out that the reason only has to *relate* to capability, qualifications or conduct, so that failing an aptitude test could relate to capability or qualifications. Similarly the Court of Appeal in *Abernethy* v. *Mott, Hay & Anderson* [1974] I.C.R. 323 held that inflexibility and lack of adaptability come within the meaning of aptitude and mental qualities. The NIRC has had more often to emphasise the breadth of "other substantial reason," holding that it does not have to be *eiusdem generis* with the rest (*R.S. Components Ltd.* v. *Irwin* [1973] I.C.R. 535) and that it need only be a reason which *could* justify dismissal, not one which *did* justify it (*Mercia Rubber Mouldings Ltd.* v. *Lingwood* [1974] I.C.R.256). Thus it is not difficult for the employer to pass this stage, especially remembering that reason (b) says conduct not misconduct.

Most cases hinge on paragraph 6(8), where the IT should

adopt "a broad approach of common sense and common fairness" (*Earl* v. *Slater & Wheeler Ltd.* [1972] I.C.R. 508) so that there are few rules. Paragraph 6(8) must always be considered, particularly in cases of redundancy (*Bessenden Properties Ltd*. v. *Corness* [1974] I.R.L.R. 338 (C.A.)) or dismissal for union activity (*Axe* v. *British Domestic Appliances Ltd.* [1973] I.C.R. 133, where there was no protection under the existing provisions specifically on union activity). In many cases no doubt the same result is reached as under the common law. Thus in a case such as *Morrish* v. *Henly's (Folkestone) Ltd.* [1973] I.C.R. 482, where the claimant was dismissed for refusing to falsify some records (though not for any dishonest purpose), the NIRC based itself on the absence of any implied term in the contract that he had to obey such an order. Lack of capability or qualifications, on the other hand, could rarely justify summary dismissal, but it must be remembered that here the question is not whether summary dismissal is justified, but whether dismissal with notice is. In a number of other important respects different results will arise.

The first is that what matters is the employer's knowledge at the time of the dismissal. As Donaldson J. said in *Earl's* case, if an employer thinks his accountant is taking money but has no real grounds for his suspicion a dismissal for this reason is unreasonable and unfair. It does not matter if it is later proved that the accountant was guilty of embezzlement. This principle may go against the claimant, as *St. Anne's Board Mill Co. Ltd.* v. *Brien* [1973] I.C.R. 444 shows. The claimants were dismissed for refusing to work with someone they believed had caused an accident. The employer's careful enquiry reached the conclusion that he had not caused the accident, but the IT reached the opposite conclusion. However, the NIRC found this irrelevant, as the employer had acted reasonably. The rule applies even though some quite different reason exists that would justify dismissal

(*W. Devis & Sons Ltd.* v. *Atkins* [1976] I.R.L.R. 16).

Similar reasoning has led to the requirement that as a general rule a claimant should be given a hearing before dismissal in order to explain his shortcomings. Again this stems from *Earl's* case where the dismissal was held unfair on this ground, for it is unreasonable to act on a reason for which there might be an explanation. Although it was said that in very rare situations there might be no sufficient explanation, the principle has been applied in very strong cases (*e.g. Munif* v. *Cole & Kirby Ltd.* [1973] I.C.R. 486, where the claimant had threatened physical violence to a director). But a brake was applied in *James* v. *Waltham Holy Cross UDC* [1973] I.C.R. 398. Donaldson J. there explained that there was not a right to a hearing in all circumstances. He contrasted *Earl's* case, where the facts were susceptible of an explanation, with at least two situations where the opportunity of an explanation may be unnecessary. One was where the claimant has already put forward a settled and considered view as part of the conduct complained of; the other was where the claimant's conduct was such that whatever the explanation his continued employment is not in the interests of the business. This does little to lessen uncertainty for it is far from clear what the interests of the business mean. Nor would it do much harm to require a hearing in all circumstances, for compensation can be refused under section 76(6) of the Employment Protection Act if the claimant in fact causes his own dismissal. Finally, although natural justice was mentioned in *Earl*, its full requirements are not imported. So the rule that a fair appeal does not remedy a defective original hearing has no application here (*Henderson* v. *Masson Scott Thrissell Engineering Ltd.* [1974] I.R.L.R. 98).

The hearing requirement was based parly also on paragraph 132 of the Code of Industrial Relations Practice, which survives for the moment at least, although it provides only a guide to be followed in ordinary cases, not binding rules (*Dacres* v. *Walls Meat Co. Ltd.* [1976] I.R.L.R. 20 on representation at hearing). Paragraph 133 suggests a disciplinary procedure, with the first step being warnings for misconduct. This led to holding that a dismissal for misconduct about which the claimant had not been warned was unfair, but always with the proviso that there was no rule of law that warnings had to be given and that everything depended on the circumstances (see *e.g. McKinney* v. *Bieganek* [1973] I.R.L.R. 311). This flexible approach was recently confirmed by the Court of Appeal in *Atkin* v. *Enfield Group Hospital Management Committee* [1975] I.R.L.R. 217, where the discretion vested in the IT is emphasised. A similar principle was applied as matter of fairness to capability (*Winterhalter Gastronom Ltd.* v. *Webb* [1973] I.C.R. 245). But there are many cases holding that express warnings were not necessary because the claimant in fact knew of his failure to come up to the mark (*e.g. Lewis Shops Group* v. *Wiggins* [1973] I.C.R. 335). It all seems to depend on whether the IT thinks the claimant could have performed better if he knew better what was demanded of him.

Much the same flexible attitude has governed other parts of the Code that have come up. The suggestion in paragraph 133 that dismissal should not follow a first breach of discipline except in the case of gross misconduct was raised in *Dalton* v. *Burton's Gold Medal Biscuits Ltd.* [1974] I.R.L.R. 45. The claimant falsified a clock card, not for personal gain or fraud. The contract of employment stated that this would result in instant dismissal, and, despite his 22 years' service, the claimant was dismissed. At common law the case would be clear, but the NIRC did not pay much attention to the contract except as a warning. However, they refused to define gross misconduct, and would not disturb the IT's finding of fair dismissal. The weight to be given to such a regulation may depend on whether it is enforced or ignored, as *Wilcox* v.

HGS Ltd. [1975] I.C.R. 333 shows, where the IT found that higher management did not condone failure to carry out safety tests on gas conversions, although such tests were often omitted. Phillips J. would not interfere with the finding of fairness. The sections about redundancy procedure seem to have been more rigorously applied. So in *Clarkson International Tools Ltd.* v. *Short* [1973] I.C.R. 191 the absence of prior consultation made dismissal unfair, and in *Vokes Ltd.* v. *Bear* [1974] I.C.R. 1 failure to try to find the claimant an alternative job made dismissal unfair. These decisions and the possibility of general unfairness have widened the statutory rule of unfairness for breach of an agreed procedure or customary arrangement. The latter has to be so well-known and certain as to amount to an "implied agreed procedure," according to *Bessenden Properties Ltd.* v. *Corness* [1973] I.R.L.R. 365. However, the *Vokes* rule is limited to redundancy situations. An attempt to extend it to dismissal for incapability through illness failed in *MANWEB* v. *Taylor* [1975] I.C.R. 185, where O'Connor J. emphasised that each case must be considered individually. There will be some circumstances in which it will be unreasonable for the employer not to attempt to find other work, and some in which it will not be. The general question of when sickness justifies dismissal is one for the IT. To do so it does not have to be so serious as to amount to a frustration of the contract (*Tan* v. *Berry Bros.* [1974] I.C.R. 586).

It might seem that these developments allow a claimant who is guilty of misconduct to obtain just as much compensation as the innocent because of a procedural defect. However, section 76(6) of the Employment Protection Act secures that this does not happen by providing that where "the dismissal was to any extent caused or contributed to by any action of the complainant it shall reduce the amount of the compensatory award by such proportion as it considers just and equitable having regard to that finding." This section replaces the previous formulation, which had given rise to intricate difficulties of interpretation, stemming from *Earl's* case. Although the courts had more or less resolved these, it is preferable to have a new start. Thus, any misconduct by the claimant which influences the decision to dismiss may result in a reduction in compensation, regardless of the fact that the misconduct has not contributed to the unfairness of dismissal (*e.g.* in failing to give a hearing or warnings). One would imagine that the word "action" could extend to other kinds of behaviour, like incapability, were it not for the statement in *Morrish* v. *Henly's* that contribution imports some element of blameworthiness. Other situations in which it seems unfair for the claimant to receive full compensation (*e.g.* failure to consult about redundancy) cannot possibly be brought within section 76(6). Such cases, and probably everything except misconduct, must be dealt with in the initial calculation of compensation under section 76(1). However, as will be seen, the new form of words here could cause problems.

Despite these complications of law, the IT has a good deal more flexibility than the common law in dealing with misconduct. In the common law, it is all or nothing; the dismissal is either wrongful or not. Here compensation can be reduced in proportion to contribution, and this helps explain the much wider definitions of when dismissal is not justified coupled with the extension in other ways of grounds which do justify it.

Redundancy Payments

A payment can only be made if the claimant is dismissed by reason of redundancy, *i.e.* if the dismissal is "attributable wholly or mainly to —

   (*a*) the fact that his employer has ceased, or intends to cease, to carry on business for the purposes for which the employee was employed by him, or has ceased, or intends to cease, to carry on that business in the place where the employee was so employed, or

(b) the fact that the requirements of that business for employees to carry out work of a particular kind, or for employees to carry out work of a particular kind in the place where they were so employed have ceased or diminished or are expected to cease or diminish.'' (Redundancy Payments Act 1965, s.1(2)).

Any dismissal is presumed to be by reason of redundancy (s.9(2)(b)), so that it is for the employer, or the Department of Employment, to show that something other than redundancy was the reason.

Thus the legal definition is somewhat narrower than the popular one, which would concentrate on the fact that the particular claimant was no longer required. The Act concentrates on the requirements of the business and has thereby produced many problems. For instance, the definition of the place of employment has been much disputed, but it is now settled that it covers any place where the claimant could contractually be required to work (*Sutcliffe* v. *Hawker Siddeley Aviation Ltd.* [1973] I.C.R. 560). Equally treacherous is the definition of the particular kind of work. The NIRC has said that it means "work which is distinguished from other work of the same general kind by requiring special aptitudes, skill or knowledge" (*Amos* v. *Max-Arc Ltd.* [1973] I.C.R. 46), but this is no great help in deciding particular cases. It is clear that the terms and conditions of employment may change considerably while the kind of work remains the same. So in *North Riding Garages Ltd.* v. *Butterwick* [1967] 2 Q.B. 56 a garage manager who could not cope with new administrative duties was held not to be dismissed for redundancy. Nor was the craftsman in *Hindle* v. *Percival Boats Ltd.* [1969] 1 All E.R. 836 who was too good and too slow for working on fibreglass rather than wooden boats. An employer may reorganise his workforce for more efficiency and a consequent dismissal is not necessarily for redundancy. All this has most recently been confirmed by the Court of Appeal in *Johnson* v. *Notts. Police Authority* [1974] I.C.R. 170. There the claimant's working hours were re-arranged, in the interests of efficiency. But if the underlying reason for the reorganisation is redundancy a payment must be made. Similarly, if the reorganisation results in a cut-down in numbers of staff, as in *Kykot* v. *Smith Hartley Ltd.* [1975] I.R.L.R. 372, or in diminished requirements for a particular kind of work. The diminution of requirements need not be for the claimant's own kind of work. If someone else is displaced and given the claimant's job, this "bumping" is due to redundancy (*W. Gimber & Sons Ltd.* v. *Spurrett* [1967] I.T.R. 308).

The result is that a group whom most laymen would say were redundant — those unable to keep up with technical advance — are denied payments. Partly this is due to rather insensitive interpretation of "work of a particular kind," but mainly it is due to the crude equation of redundancy with surplus of labour in the Act. The Act is meant to encourage efficiency, but the definition denies payments to these victims of greater efficiency and as such is at odds with its overall policy. However, the incoherence of this policy is shown by arguments that allowing a payment would discourage employers from pursuing efficiency (see Sachs L.J. in *Hindle's* case at p.843). In fact, only 11 per cent. of managers in the 1969 survey thought that the Act had made it more difficult to dismiss workers (Parker and Thomas, p.62).

Thus it is clear that dismissal for incompetence, age or misconduct is not dismissal for redundancy. This is so even though there is a redundancy situation and even though the employer is mistaken in his opinion about the claimant. According to *Hindle's* case all that matters is the reason which genuinely motivated the employer, no matter how capricious. The objections to this rule have lessened with the introduction of the unfair dismissal legislation, but a claimant may still be adversely affected.

It is worth noting that the fact that redundancy is "self-induced" is in itself irrelevant. So if industrial action leads to reduced business, *Sanders* v. *Ernest A. Neale* [1974] I.C.R. 565 says that this does not disentitle anyone involved from a payment. The question is whether the redundancy situation causes the dismissal, or some other reason, such as refusing to work normally, as in *Sanders* v. *Neale*. The NIRC further suggests that the obscure section 2(2) of the Redundancy Payments Act applies where dismissal is due to redundancy, but the employer would be entitled to dismiss the claimant without notice. Depending on the notice given the claimant loses his right to a payment. The section is rarely needed in view of *Hindle*. For the full complexities see Hepple and O'Higgins, pp.152-155.

Unemployment Benefit

A claimant may be disqualified for benefit for not more than six weeks if "he has lost his employment through his misconduct, or has voluntarily left such employment without just cause" (National Insurance Act 1965, s.22(2), Social Security Act 1975, s.20(1)(*a*)). Around these simple phrases, which first appeared in the National Insurance Act 1911, has grown up a complex body of rules, developed first by the Umpires and then by the National Insurance Commissioners.

They have established some principles common to both disqualifications. The first is that the primary object is not to penalise the claimant, but more to discourage avoidable claims against the National Insurance Fund. To use Kempfer's terms, the causal theory has been adopted. "The basic purpose of unemployment benefit is to provide against the misfortune of unemployment happening against a person's will'' (R(U) 20/64). It is sometimes said that this is the equivalent of the principle of insurance law denying indemnity for events wilfully caused by the insured (see Sanders, p.308). Indeed, this was mentioned in R(U) 17/54, but it was said that the application of the principle was limited. Since it is clear that some voluntary unemployment is to be covered, a test of reasonableness in relation to the rest of the community has evolved: the claimant must do what is reasonable to avoid becoming a charge on the Fund. Any ascription of purpose to the scheme is of course a creative act, but these principles are so settled as to be beyond challenge.

Further evidence for the causal theory is that the maximum disqualification is six weeks. The justification for this departure from the voluntary unemployment principle is that six weeks is roughly the amount of unemployment that can be attributed to an initial act of misconduct. Any more can be said to be due to general labour conditions, as can be tested by other provisions on availability and refusing suitable work. It appeared settled that six weeks is the normal disqualification, only to be reduced if special circumstances are shown (R(U) 17/54), but a Tribunal of Commissioners has in R(U) 8/74 affirmed that the authorities are fettered by no such presumptions and that the period should be fixed according to the merits of the particular case. There is thus considerable flexibility and the Tribunal recognises that differences in treatment will arise.

Leaving voluntarily

Once it is shown that the claimant left his job voluntarily, it is then for him to show that he had just cause (C.U. 16/66). Thus the first question is what leaving voluntarily means. There are few decisions on the situation where the claimant leaves following repudiatory conduct by the employer. Here, in contrast to unfair dismissal, etc., the issue has usually been dealt with as one of justness of cause. Only where the claimant did no more than anticipate an inevitable dismissal was he said not to be acting voluntarily (R(U) 1/58). More authority governs the converse situation where the employer terminates the contract, but the claimant is held in effect to have left voluntarily. The rule is that if a person deliberately and knowingly acts in a way which makes it necessary for the employer to dismiss him, he may be regarded as leaving voluntarily. In the leading decision, the claimant refused to submit to an X-ray which was a condition of employment (R(U) 16/52), but later cases were even weaker, like R(U) 18/57 where the claimant refused to do work he was not contractually required to do. Indeed in C.U. 2/68, the Commissioner, while not questioning the principle of provoking dismissal, said that it was too much relied on. The claimant refused to transfer to a new place of work when the old one was closing down. This was held to be a genuine disagreement about the terms of a new contract, and quite different from provocation. This approach, following that of R(U) 9/59 (dismissal for refusing to join superannuation scheme, not voluntarily leaving — claimant had genuine objection) stresses the intentions of the claimant, as inferred from his actions. A recent decision (R(U) 7/74) develops this, suggesting that normally the claimant's action must amount to a deliberate repudiation of the contract. Although the basic principle was not questioned, the Commissioner said that he did not know what "necessary to dismiss" meant in the formulation of the rule in R(U) 16/52. A more contractual approach would be welcome for it would prevent attempts to evade limitations on disqualification for misconduct by arguing that the claimant provoked dismissal.

However, these complications are rare. Mostly the claimant simply terminates the contract. Then the question is whether he had just cause. The principle was set out in R(U) 20/64. "It is not sufficient for the claimant to prove that he acted reasonably, in the sense of acting reasonably in his own interests. The interests of the National Insurance Fund and other contributors must be taken into account as well. 'The notion of 'just cause' involves a compromise between the rights of the individual and the interests of the rest of the community. So long as he does not break his contract with his employer, the individual is free to leave his employment when he likes. But if he wishes to claim unemployment benefit he must not leave his employment without due regard to the interests of the rest of the community ...' (C.U. 164/50).'' Thus the question is not what a reasonable man would have done, but a more abstract and general one, which the Commissioners are reluctant to tie down by too many generalisations. In R(U) 4/70 the phrase "just cause" was said to be undefinable, but intended to allow the authorities to decide each case on its merits.

Nonetheless, certain guidelines have been laid down. First, the claimant should as a rule have some definite engagement in other employment, though not necessarily following immediately (C.U. 5/71 — break of week to organise as self-employed reasonable). Nor need the job materialise if it was reasonably expected (C.U. 23/68). Taking a greater chance may be reasonable if the current employment is precarious, as it was in R(U) 4/73. There the claimant had the chance of a secure job, which did not materialise until he had been unemployed for three weeks. He was not disqualified. A similar approach was taken to the claimant who resigned after six weeks of trial employment without having found a new job (R(U) 3/73). However, less scope is allowed to the claimant whose reason for putting himself on the National Insurance Fund is a grievance against his employer. It is said that he may have good cause for leaving *vis-à-vis* the employer, but it does not necessarily follow that there is good cause *vis-à-vis* the Fund. He should submit his grievance to the grievance procedure covering his job or refer it to his trade union, rather than leave immediately (R(U) 33/51). But that case was one where the employees were trying to alter the terms of the contract. The rule has not yet been applied in a reported case where it is the employer who goes outside the contract. This was enough in itself in R(U) 18/57 but other cases have needed special circumstances. In R(U) 15/53 these were that the claimant was given no time to consider the new and lower wage-rates imposed by the employer and in C.U. 9/70 the claimant's youth and inexperience and the fact that he had no trade union help (even then he was disqualified for a nominal period). It is hard to believe that the reasonable man would consider these borderline cases of just cause, independent of the Commissioners' gloss of balancing interests. Perhaps C.U. 7/75 presages a more flexible approach. There the claimant complained to a foreman about the incorrect loading of his lorry, but was told to take it or leave it. The Commissioner decided that this was a sufficient attempt to get the grievance remedied to constitute just cause for leaving.

Certainly the approach contrasts with that towards the claimant who left rather than join a union (R(U) 38/53). It was said that his action would be disapproved of by his workmates, and that it was unreasonable to expect him to continue working in an intolerable atmosphere, so that there was just cause. This might be upheld on the ground that the whole job became unsuitable (like R(U) 3/73 or R(U) 40/53 — waiter forced to peel potatoes) rather than an isolated grievance arising, but the line between these two categories is very thin. Reliance was placed on the claimant's right to join or not to join a union, but equally a claimant has a right not to have his contract broken. I consider that the union membership approach should be more generally applied, although it may be that the discretion to reduce the period of disqualification is enough.

Personal circumstances may justify leaving, providing that they are sufficiently pressing. There are many cases about

policemen who retire at the most advantageous age for
pension purposes. It is clear that personal financial advantage
is not enough, although when linked to the need for capital to
provide for dependants and the difficulty in securing another
job in employment, it might justify leaving (see R(U)
4/70). But the same case points out that all the individual
circumstances must be considered, including the availability
of alternative provision for dependants and the amount of
job-hunting done. Thus most policemen are disqualified, but
for reduced periods. There are any number of personal or
domestic reasons which may suffice. Examples are, leaving to
be with dying father (R(U) 32/59); leaving to move with wife
and baby from two attic rooms to a house (R(U) 31/59);
leaving to avert a nervous breakdown (C.U. 16/72). But here
discretion is free, so that any circumstances *may* do.

Misconduct

Misconduct has been defined as "simply such misconduct as
would leave a reasonable employer to terminate a claimant's
employment, whether with or without notice" (R(U) 24/55).
As a definition this is question-begging, although it is further
evidence for the causal theory: misconduct is putting oneself
on the Fund in a way which is avoidable. But it is not any
conduct which makes the employer dismiss the claimant,
otherwise few would ever receive benefit. There must be an
element of blameworthiness, of fault. Misconduct "may be
constituted by mere carelessness; but in considering whether a
person has been guilty of misconduct it is necessary to
discriminate between that type and degree of carelessness
which may have to be put up with in human affairs, and the
more deliberate or more serious type of carelessness which
justifies withholding unemployment benefit because the
employee has lost his employment through his own avoidable
fault" (R(U) 8/57). Nor is it enough that the employer
considers that the claimant is guilty of misconduct. The

authorities must make up their own minds, and the findings of other bodies are merely evidence. The answer to a different legal question is not binding, but a finding of fact by a court will be cogent evidence, as will be a finding by an IT on an unfair dismissal claim. R(U) 2/74 confirms that the authorities are free to take a different view of the facts even here. Although any evidence is admissible, misconduct must be clearly proved, preferably by direct evidence if the claimant contests the issue (R(U) 2/60).

Thus misconduct is regarded as a serious allegation. Trivial errors, such as allowing one frost-fire to go out in a night (R(U) 2/60), or working too slowly, but as fast as the claimant could (R(U) 34/52, will not do. It is more difficult to generalise about what will amount to misconduct. Absence without leave or without taking reasonable steps to inform the employer if sick usually does (R(U) 1/57). If the claimant fears to tell the employer that he is taking time off to look for a new job this will mitigate the misconduct to cut down the period of disqualification (R(U) 8/61). Refusal to obey a reasonable order is misconduct, unless there are reasonable grounds for refusal. This was stated in R(U) 35/58, where the claimant refused to work compulsory overtime, but no clue was given as to what would justify refusal. Similarly a breach of the employer's rules, providing it is not trivial, is misconduct (R(U) 24/56 — breach of Post Office rule against staff betting by post).

Union action is rarely recognised as justifying disobedience. Certainly if the claimant ignores a collectively agreed grievance procedure he has little hope. In R(U) 41/53 a crane driver refused to operate a crane on a jetty when a dispute had been declared at a lunch-time meeting after hazard money was withdrawn by the employers. There was no attempt to use the procedure for settling disputes. He was dismissed for misconduct. This is a clear sanction for collectively agreed standards, but these standards are not always upheld. In C.U.

4/67 a works convener was dismissed after visiting a part of the factory contrary to management orders. An agreement provided that consent should not be unreasonably withheld for such visits and there was strong evidence that here consent was unreasonably withheld. But the Commissioner was not concerned whether the agreement had been broken, relying on the fact that the terms of the collective agreement were not incorporated into the claimant's contract of employment. The case was regarded as one where the claimant had deliberately disobeyed the employer's instructions, which was clearly misconduct. This decision must be doubtful, for if departure from a collective agreement is relevant to the claimant's misconduct, it must also be relevant to the reasonableness of the employer's order. In particular, the non-incorporation into the individual contracts is irrelevant to the factual question of misconduct.

Criminal offences during employment are always misconduct, even stealing an apparently abandoned piece of sacking worth 1/4d. (R(U) 190/50). Conduct not proved to be criminal may be such serious carelessness as to be misconduct. This was so in R(U) 8/57 where a shop manager could not explain cash shortages. Offences outside employment raise more problems. If a conviction makes it impossible for employment to continue, *e.g.* a driver disqualified from driving, the act leading to it amounts to misconduct (R(U) 7/57), unless the claimant can show that he was innocent of the necessary degree of blame (R(U) 24/64). This might be so if the conviction was for an offence of strict liability. Other sorts of convictions are subject to the same rules as any conduct outside working hours. The decision depends on whether the conduct so affects the suitability of the claimant for his employment that a reasonable employer would dismiss him. Cases suggest that any offence of dishonesty automatically makes the claimant unsuitable, so that in R(U) 20/59 an apprentice draughtsman put on probation for breaking into premises was guilty of misconduct. This is reminiscent of the common law approach, but may be unrealistic in modern industrial situations.

In other situations a more direct connection with the job is necessary. In R(U) 14/57 the claimant lodged in a customer's premises and was dismissed after a complaint from the customer about the claimant's drunkenness on their premises outside working hours. This was misconduct, for what a man does in his own time is not his concern alone, although the special circumstance of the incident taking place on the customer's premises was clearly important here. In more recent cases, concerning sexual offences, a more thorough investigation has been made of whether the claimant becomes unsuitable for the particular job. The fullest discussion is in R(U) 1/71 which concerned a local authority gardener who was convicted of committing an act of gross indecency with another man. It was recognised that in many cases such an offence would be irrelevant to a job, but the claimant was held to have sufficient opportunity to embarrass the public, despite not being employed in a public park, for this to amount to misconduct. However, since the connection was so tenuous only a week's disqualification was imposed. Everything must depend on the precise circumstances, so that in a similar case involving an inspector in a factory whose workmates all knew of the offence, there was no effect on suitability (C.U. 8/70). However, there is a slightly disturbing passage in R(U) 1/71 where it is suggested that in some employments, *e.g.* as a school teacher or government employee, the employer may have a legitimate interest in his employees' maintaining a high standard of conduct at all times. It is not clear if this is limited to sexual offences, but even so it seems an undesirably general rule.

It should be noted that actions before the particular employment began (even criminal acts) cannot constitute misconduct (R(U) 1/58). This is presumably because the claimant cannot be blameworthy in relation to a job not yet in existence. In this respect the rules are more liberal than in other systems. Similarly, if the employer waives his right to dismiss for misconduct a subsequent dismissal cannot be said to occur through that misconduct (C.U. 4/72).

The misconduct does not have to be the sole cause of the loss of employment. In R(U) 14/57 the employers had additional reasons for dismissing the claimant, since he had led unofficial strikes, but since the misconduct was the final reason for dismissal, it occurred *through* misconduct. This is the inevitable result of the concentration on the claimant's conduct, for if the claimant can foresee that his action will lead to dismissal it is likely to be misconduct. However, it may be that in the light of the unfair dismissal legislation more attention will be paid to the reasonableness of the employer's action. This was mooted in C.U. 16/73, where the Commissioner recognised that ITs are developing a new industrial morality and finding employers' behaviour unreasonable in circumstances in which that would not previously have been suggested. The National Insurance authorities would have to take account of this new morality, possibly in holding that claimants have lost employment not through misconduct, but through a combination of their conduct and their employer's unreasonableness. It remains to be seen how far this important initiative will be taken up by the other Commissioners. Potentially, the requirements of warnings and hearings could be incorporated. For the moment, the main effect may be on the length of disqualification, now that it is being emphasised that the whole context of the dismissal should be considered. There is no limitation to mitigating circumstances in the nature of the misconduct, as was suggested in R(U) 27/52 (C.U. 16/73 and 7/74).

Supplementary Benefit

The approach of the SBC is straightforward and severe. Under paragraph 11 of Schedule 2 to the Supplementary Benefit Act 1966 (added in 1971) the benefit of a claimant who is disqualified for unemployment benefit for misconduct or leaving voluntarily is reduced by 40 per cent. of the single person's rate. Thus increases for dependants and rents remain intact, but a deduction of, at current rates, £4.36 from a subsistence level of income is a substantial matter. The deduction applies only to those required to register for work, but extends to anyone who would be disqualified if he applied for unemployment benefit regardless of whether he has not claimed or a claim has been disallowed on other grounds. If a claim is made, either the insurance officer's decision or his opinion that he would have imposed the disqualification can be followed. However, if no claim was made, the SBC has to decide what the insurance officer would do, which is not entirely satisfactory.

The SBC recognises the potential harshness of this provision, for officials are instructed to be on the alert for hardship if a long disqualification is imposed (Handbook, para.200). Some examples are given: where the claimant's last job was short-lived or low-paid in relation to his commitments; where his wife is pregnant or there are very young children; where there are unmet housing or HP costs which cannot be met from disregarded income; or if there is sickness or some unusual difficulty. However, it is only in very exceptional circumstances that any less than 75p (the pre-1971 figure) will be deducted.

The result is to reinforce the sanctions contained in the unemployment benefit system. This might appear penal, but since levels of unemployment benefit have generally been below those of supplementary benefit, it is thought that some deduction is necessary otherwise disqualification would have no effect on the claimant at all.

Chapter 5

BENEFITS

How is compensation calculated when a claimant is entitled to it? Is the benefit flat-rate or is there an attempt to make full restitution of what has been lost? How far is benefit primary or secondary, *i.e.* is it reduced if compensation is received from another source? In many ways these questions are at the heart of "the system," and the differing answers, particularly to the last, expose the fragmented and uncoordinated approach to the problem of unemployment. Further, although the trend is away from flat-rate benefits, there are differences in how near to full restitution each benefit goes. Here there is a clear progression from the approach in an unfair dismissal, which has greatly widened the narrow common law approach, to that in the social security system, with its limited extension from the flat-rate principle only for unemployment benefit. It is interesting to link these differences in treatment to one of the issues raised in the last chapter: of what it is about some claimants which merits more generous treatment, why some claimants are more deserving than others. For these connections see the Conclusion.

Wrongful Dismissal
The purpose of damages for breach of any contract is to put the injured party as far as possible in the position he would have been in if the contract had been performed; straight-forwardly restitutionary. In the case of contracts of

employment damages will normally be the amount of wages the claimant would have received during the period of proper notice. This is held to be the only legal expectation. The employer could have ended the contract legally by giving that length of notice. So if the claimant is entitled only to short notice, the common law offers little protection. Further, it was established by the House of Lords in *Addis* v. *Gramophone Co. Ltd.* [1909] A.C. 488 that damages are not recoverable for the manner of the dismissal, whether it injures prestige or future prospects. The rule is harsh, for there is certainly a general feeling that there is something derogatory about being summarily dismissed, or even being given wages in lieu of notice. The difficulty a particular worker may have in getting another job can be a factor in determining the length of notice he is entitled to, but this is no help when the difficulty stems from the manner of dismissal. However, the recent decision in *Cox* v. *Philips Industries* [1975] I.R.L.R. 344 has confused the situation. There Lawson J. gave the plaintiff, who had been transferred in breach of contract to a useless job, £500 damages for the consequent distress and frustration. He was able to avoid *Addis* because the plaintiff was not dismissed at the time of the breach, although technically, as has been seen, that is how the situation ought to be analysed. Thus it is not clear how far *Cox* makes an inroad into the *Addis* principle itself. In some exceptional cases damages can be given for loss of the opportunity to work. Thus in *Clayton* v. *Oliver* [1930] A.C. 209 an actor got damages for loss of the chance to enhance his reputation, but the limits of this rule are hard to define. Other cases suggest that it may be a breach of contract for the employer not to supply work, but this does not necessarily mean that additional damages are payable on wrongful dismissal. One genuine exception is that apprentices may claim for loss of future prospects as a qualified man if their contract is prematurely ended (*Dunk* v. *Waller & Son Ltd.* [1970] 2 Q.B.

163).

The amount of compensation may include sums to which there is no right, providing the loss of those other benefits is reasonably contemplated by both parties. So the hairdresser in *Manubens* v. *Leon* [1919] 1 K.B. 208 was entitled to a sum representing tips lost in the period of notice. According to Lush J. it was an implied term of the contract that the employer would not prevent the employee from recovering sums he would ordinarily receive if he was working. However, the limits are shown by *Lavarack* v. *Woods of Colchester Ltd* [1967] 1 Q.B. 278, where the Court of Appeal held that a dismissed director was not entitled to the amount of increased salary which he would have received when the defendants discontinued their discretionary bonus scheme. He was entitled to the bonus to the end of the year for which it had already been settled. This follows the principle that the court should assume that the defendant would have performed his obligations in the way least burdensome to himself. Thus, in general some legal obligation is necessary, but there may be exceptions. Diplock L.J. pointed out that the court should not assume that discretionary benefits would be withdrawn from the plaintiff if that would involve countervailing disadvantages in relation to other employees. Thus in *Bold* v. *Brough, Nicholson & Hall Ltd.* [1964] 1 W.L.R. 201 a pension scheme could only be discontinued as a whole, so the plaintiff recovered the benefit of the employer's contributions, whereas in *Beach* v. *Read Corrugated Cases Ltd.* [1956] 1 W.L.R. 807 the employers were able to discontinue contributions to the plaintiff alone and the opposite result was reached. Perhaps the principle could be used to argue that, as well as overtime which the employer is under a legal obligation to provide, "discretionary" overtime should be counted for common law damages.

The principle of compensation leads to a further rule that the worker should not receive more in damages than he would actually have received if he was working. Specifically, what would have been deducted for income tax and Social Security contributions is also deducted so that the worker does not get the "windfall" of the full contractual sum. The windfall instead goes to the employer. No liability to tax or contribution is incurred, so no money is actually transferred to the government. However, the principle was established for income tax in *British Transport Commission* v. *Gourley* [1956] A.C. 185. This was a personal injuries case, but the same principles are recognised as applying to wrongful dismissal. The House of Lords decided that if the earnings lost were taxable and the damages were not, then the employer need only pay in damages the amount of earnings reduced by the amount of tax that would have been paid on them. The fact that this involved hypothetical calculations was brushed aside, although the House was prepared to take account of the way in which the worker was likely to arrange his affairs so as to minimise his tax liability. The result was that damages of £37,720 were reduced to £6,695.

This was at least relatively simple to apply, but in 1960 the Finance Act (ss.37-38, Sched.13; now Income and Corporation Taxes Act 1970, ss.187-188) made "any payment (not otherwise chargeable to tax) which is made ... in consideration or in consequence of, or otherwise in connection with, the termination of the holding of the office or employment" subject to tax in the hands of the recipient. Sums up to £5,000 were then to be exempt from tax. The main purpose was to tax large golden handshakes to executives but the Act also applied to wrongful dismissal damages. The effect of the Act was first raised in England in *Parsons* v. *BNM Laboratories Ltd.*, which concerned damages of £1,200 gross. Master Jacob ((1962) 106 Sol. Jo. 736) held simply that the Act had removed damages for wrongful dismissal from the purview of the court and the *Gourley* rule. Damages were now liable to tax, so that one of the *Gourley* conditions was not fulfilled.

However, the Court of Appeal ([1964] 1 Q.B. 95) could not accept this attractive and logical conclusion. By a majority, they decided that the class of payments subject to tax was not "all payments" but only those over £5,000. Since payments under £5,000 were not taxable *Gourley* still applied to them and £320 was deducted from the damages. The problem was what happened when the gross sum was over £5,000 and the court made some suggestions. It is really no good to say that if the amount is over £5,000 then *Gourley* does not apply at all, for that would lead to enormous differences according to whether the amount was just below or just above the limit. Nor will the over-simplified rule that *Parsons* is often quoted for do. This is what Phillimore J. did in *Bold* v. *Brough, Nicolson & Hall* (*supra*) (and apparently Crichton J. in *Basnett* v. *J.&A. Jackson Ltd.* [1976] I.C.R. 63). On a gross award of £25,000 he took the first £5,000 and calculated the *Gourley* deduction on it, estimating it on the lowest slice of income and spread over the whole period for which damages were awarded. The deduction came to £800, which was simply knocked off the amount of damages. This will not do because it gives the claimant more than his actual loss, which is to be avoided if *Gourley* is going to be involved at all. For the claimant is taxed on the amount he actually receives and the *Gourley* deduction reduces the slice of the award over £5,000. To take a simple example: a gross award of £8,000, assuming the *Gourley* tax rate to be 30 per cent. (forgetting about personal allowances, etc.). Applying *Gourley* to the lot leaves £5,600, which is assumed to be the actual loss. Applying *Gourley* to the bottom £5,000 leaves £3,500 and the claimant gets the slice over £5,000 (*i.e.* £3,000) intact. Total £6,500, out of which the claimant pays tax on £1,500. He will have to pay tax at a fair bit higher rate than the *Gourley* one to reduce that amount to £600. If the rates are the same (the usual situation) then he ends up with a total of £6,000.

The approach in fact preferred in *Parsons* was to apply

Gourley to the gross sum. If the result is over £5,000 then the gross sum is awarded; if it is below then that is the award. However, this still leaves anomalies between awards just on opposite sides of the line, so the tax books approve a departure from *Parsons* if the post-*Gourley* amount is over £5,000. This is to take the remaining slice over £5,000 and gross it up by adding back the tax deducted from it. To take the £8,000 gross damages again. The post-*Gourley* sum is £5,600. The excess of £600 represents approximately £859 taxed at 30 per cent. The final award should therefore be £5,859. The result is that if the claimant is taxed on the damages at the *Gourley* rate the amount he actually receives will equal his actual loss. He loses if the rate is higher. It might be said that this negates the effect of the Act, but is probably the fairest way of integrating *Gourley* with it, although I prefer Master Jacob's straightforward solution. There is the further disadvantage that there is no authority for this method of calculation although it can be regarded as an extension of the *Parsons* rule. The result is a considerable mess, which is why I have taken some time to sort it out. It is surprising that so few cases are reported. One can only conclude that the parties prefer to agree these matters. In line with this unshakeable rule of precise compensation, the amount of Social Security contributions the claimant would have had to make are also deducted (*Cooper* v. *Firth Brown Ltd.* [1963] 1 W.L.R. 418).

The other side of the principle is that the defendant may be able to deduct money received by the claimant from other sources. Any earnings from employment are to be deducted. As a result of the rule that the claimant must take reasonable steps to mitigate his loss, if he unreasonably fails to get a job what he could have earned can also be deducted. This will be explored further in the chapter on Neglect of Job Opportunities, but here I can say if there are many vacancies in the labour market the duty to mitigate can almost destroy the effectiveness of the remedy of damages. The court in *Parsons* v. *BNM* held that any unemployment benefit received must be deducted and the rule has been applied several times since by the Court of Appeal (*Dunk* v. *Waller* [1970] 2 Q.B. 163, *Cheeseman* v. *Bowaters Ltd.* [1971] 1 W.L.R. 1773). The rule seems settled at that level, but there are grave doubts on the reasoning behind it. In *Parsons* different reasons were given, none convincing, for rejecting Master Jacob's analogy to payments under an insurance policy held by the claimant. According to Sellers L.J. the worker alone pays the premium for an insurance policy, while in the case of a pension arising from employment his services under the contract are equivalent to the premium. But he considered that "where, as here, the employer has made a contribution to the unemployment insurance he should get the benefit of it, if he finds it necessary to put one of his employees into unemployment, even in circumstances where he is liable to compensate him in damages" ([1964] 1 Q.B. 121). It has already been argued that the employer's contribution is in reality paid by the worker, but more importantly *Parry* v. *Cleaver* [1970] A.C. 1 has exploded the view that benefits contributed to by the employer must be deducted. Lords Reid and Wilberforce in particular view the payment of a pension as a reward for past service, regardless of exactly how the contributions are distributed between employer and worker. The approach of Pearson and Harman L.JJ., to ask if the benefits were collateral and too remote to be deducted is too simplistic to survive either. *Parry* v. *Cleaver* requires a considerably deeper examination of the issues. It is true that there is no statement of public policy, like that in the Fatal Accidents Act on non-deduction of pensions, to turn to in the wrongful dismissal field, but the basis of the *Parsons* decision seems undermined.

Certainly, there is now a good deal of confusion over the principles to be applied. In *Hewson* v. *Downs* [1970] 1 Q.B.

73 a retirement pension (financed on a tripartite basis) was not deducted from personal injury damages. *Foxley* v. *Olton* [1965] 2 Q.B. 306 holds that supplementary benefit (then National Assistance) is not to be deducted, yet Lord Reid in *Parry* v. *Cleaver* thought provisionally that the same rule should govern both this and unemployment benefit. He did not say which rule. In *Basnett* v. *J. & A. Jackson* (*supra*) supplementary benefit was not deducted, while unemployment benefit was. In *Hartley* v. *Sandholme Iron Co. Ltd.* [1975] Q.B. 600 Nield J. deducted the amount of an income tax refund from personal injury damages, saying he was following *Gourley*. Arnold J. has decided in *Stocks* v. *Magna Merchants Ltd.* [1973] 1 W.L.R. 1505 that a redundancy payment must be deducted from wrongful dismissal damages, holding that it was more closely analogous to unemployment benefit in terms of remoteness. The decision is clearly wrong, and has indeed been differed from in the *Basnett* case and the unfair dismissal context. Here one of the alternative arguments in *Parry* v. *Cleaver* is useful. This is to ask if the benefit is intended to be kept by the claimant regardless of other sources of compensation (*i.e.* is it primary, rather than secondary?). The police disability pension there was payable irrespective of what other income the claimant received. Therefore it could be said that it was introduced to benefit the claimant not the wrongdoer. A redundancy payment is made on dismissal for redundancy, regardless of whether unemployment follows. Its purpose is not directly to replace lost income as its calculation indicates. Therefore it should not be deducted. It has been suggested (see Cooper) that this reasoning is the, or the desirable, principle to be derived from *Parry* v. *Cleaver*. I think it clear that in fact the separate reasons were regarded as cumulative, each on its own sufficient for the decision, yet it might be feasible to grade different benefits according as their conditions make them primary or secondary. This would mean that both

unemployment benefit and supplementary benefit would be deducted from wrongful dismissal damages, for both abate if the claimant is receiving payments to replace wages. However, I would prefer to stress the importance of public policy, which may require different principles to be applied to wrongful dismissal claims than to personal injury cases. The imposition of damages in this area may still have a deterrent effect on employers. The doctrine of mitigation and short notice periods already weaken the remedy so much that unfair dismissal legislation was necessary. If other benefits (particularly redundancy payments) are also deducted it means that an employer might be able to get away with a wrongful dismissal absolutely free. He should not be able to collect *all* the windfalls. There are still situations where unfair dismissal protection is not available, so the issue is important. The Employment Protection Act contains a provision (s.112) which allows regulations to be made under which the government may recoup unemployment benefit and supplementary benefit from an employer. However, this can only apply to payments which are the subject of proceedings before an Industrial Tribunal, so that wrongful dismissal damages cannot be affected until jurisdiction to deal with them is granted to ITs under section 109.

Unfair Dismissal

The Employment Protection Act contains a complicated set of rules on the calculation of compensation which have to be grafted on to the principles developed by the NIRC under the former legislation. This is partly the result of an attempt to reinforce reinstatement and re-engagement as the primary remedies for unfair dismissal. First where dismissal is for union membership or activity, the employer may be ordered to continue the claimant's contract, under sections 78-80, pending determination or settlement of the claim. But in the ordinary case the procedure is this. The IT must take into account whether the claimant wishes to be reinstated or re-engaged, whether it is practicable for the employer to comply with an order, and whether, where the claimant has caused or contributed to his dismissal, it would be just to make an order (s.71(6) and (7)). Reinstatement must be considered first, although re-engagement must be on terms which are, so far as reasonably practicable, as favourable as reinstatement, except in cases of contributory fault. In considering practicability the IT must ignore the hiring of a permanent replacement unless the employer shows, in terms of section 71(8), that it was impracticable or unreasonable not so to replace the claimant. If the employer does not comply with an order, then, unless he shows that it was impracticable to do so, he must pay between 13 and 26 weeks' pay in addition to the ordinary compensation (s.72(2)). In cases of dismissal for union reasons or by way of racial or sex discrimination this amount is from 26 to 52 weeks' pay. If the employer takes the claimant back, but does not fully comply with the order, the IT may award such compensation as it thinks fit (s.72(1)).

If no order is made, then the IT can move straight to the assessment of compensation. This is now in two parts: the basic award and the compensatory award. The basic award is the amount of the statutory redundancy payment to which the claimant would be entitled if dismissed for redundancy, or two weeks' pay if that is more (s.74). If the reason for dismissal is redundancy, then the basic award is reduced by any payment made (s.75(8)) or, if the claimant has unreasonably refused an offer of employment or is not treated as dismissed under the Redundancy Payments Act, is restricted to two weeks' pay (s.74(2)). In non-redundancy cases the amount may be reduced if the claimant caused or contributed to the dismissal (s.75(7)). The effect is that an employer will not find it cheaper to dismiss a man unfairly rather than for redundancy, and that claimants who under the NIRC rules would have got minimal compensation do get a certain amount. The compensatory award is calculated in much the same way as under the former legislation. Section 76(1) provides that it "shall be such amount as the tribunal considers just and equitable in all the circumstances having regard to the loss sustained by the complainant in consequence of the dismissal in so far as that loss is attributable to action taken by the employer." By section 76(2) loss includes any expenses reasonably incurred by the claimant in consequence of the dismissal and loss of any benefit the claimant might reasonably be expected to have had. This is subject to section 76(3), which deals with the relationship with the basic award, and section 76(4), which incorporates the common law duty to mitigate loss. The maximum amount of the compensatory award is currently £5,200 (Trade Union and Labour Relations Act 1974, Sched.1, para.20, as substituted by Employment Protection Act 1975, Sched.16, Part III, para.17).

Around the somewhat vague formula as it existed in 1971, the NIRC quickly built a sophisticated approach, which took a very wide view of benefits lost. The basis is its decision in *Norton Tool Co. Ltd.* v. *Tewson* [1972] I.C.R. 501 where four possible heads of damage were set out: (a) immediate loss of wages, *i.e.* during the notice period; (b) manner of dismissal; (c) future loss of wages; and (d) loss of protection in respect of unfair dismissal or redundancy. I will deal with each of these in turn, adding a separate category of loss of pension rights.

(a) *Immediate loss of wages*

Here the basis is that the claimant is entitled to what good industrial practice would provide. Since such practice requires at least payment of wages in lieu of notice, the amount of which cannot be affected by receipt of other earnings or benefits during the notice period, then this amount is to be paid. This is a departure from the common law, which is described as irrelevant to the interpretation of the Act. The figure is take home pay, *i.e.* net of estimated tax and Social Security contributions, without deductions for anything else. The position is confirmed most recently by *Vaughan* v. *Weighpack Ltd.* [1974] I.C.R. 261. Under this head can also be included such odds and ends as any arrears of wages, accrued holiday pay, etc.

(b) *Manner of dismissal*
Norton holds that "loss" does not include injury to pride and feelings, so that compensation is only available when the manner of dismissal gives rise to some future financial loss, *i.e.* by making re-employment less likely. *Vaughan* v. *Weighpack Ltd.* indicates that this head will be invoked only on the very rarest occasions. However, the decision in *Cox*. v. *Philips Industries* might have some influence here.

(c) *Future loss of wages*
In *Norton* only the possibility of future insecurity of employment is mentioned, for the claimant got a new job at higher wages. But in many cases the claimant takes a drop in wages or is still unemployed at the date of the hearing. Then the IT must estimate how long it will take him to regain his former level of earnings and award compensation accordingly, taking account of possible short-time working, unemployment, etc. Clearly the manner of dismissal may be relevant to this calculation, as may the upset or nervous shock which the NIRC will not compensate for directly. Probable increases of salary in the old job are relevant, in contrast to *Lavarack* v. *Woods*, although the amount is discounted for the fact that increases are only probabilities, not legal commitments (*York Trailer Ltd*. v. *Sparkes* [1973] I.C.R. 518). Loss of benefits in kind (*e.g.* use of a company car, *Nohar* v. *Granitstone Ltd.* [1974] I.C.R. 273) may be compensated.

The loss will also depend on the likelihood of the old job

continuing. The NIRC has held in a number of cases that if the claimant would probably have been dismissed if the employer had acted fairly this must be taken into account in the assessment of compensation. In *Earl* v. *Slater & Wheeler* [1972] I.C.R. 508, where the claimant had no valid explanation that could have been put forward if he had been given a hearing, the loss was put at nil, and no compensation at all awarded. In *Winterhalter Gastronom Ltd.* v. *Webb* [1973] I.C.R. 245, where the claimant was dismissed for incapability without having been warned how he was failing, the NIRC assessed the chances of his improving sufficiently to keep his job. The greater the chance, the larger the proportion of his wage loss to be awarded on top of wages for the period it would be fair to give him for improvement. A similar principle was applied in *Vokes Ltd.* v. *Bear* [1974] I.C.R. 1 where the employer made no attempt to find the redundant claimant a job. The greater the chances of finding a job, the larger the proportion of wage loss awarded. It seems that this principle can deal with most situations where a reduction for contributory fault under section 76(6) is not appropriate, and is still good despite the change in wording of the legislation. The Employment Protection Act talks of loss "in consequence of the dismissal," which is wider than the old loss "in consequence of the matters to which the complaint relates." According to *Earl* the complaint related only to the unfairness of dismissal, although in *Maris* v. *Rotheram Corporation* [1974] I.C.R. 435 a wider view was confirmed.

Under this head the NIRC has held that account must be taken of collateral benefits, for the object is to restore the claimant to his former financial position. In *Vaughan* v. *Weighpack Ltd.* it was said that all sums received as a direct consequence of dismissal must be deducted, but that may be too wide. Unemployment benefit seems to be agreed, but it is often not clear whether supplementary benefit is also deducted, for ITs often talk vaguely of "social security benefits." Since common law practice is followed here benefits." Since common law practice is followed here without much discussion of principles there is an argument for separating out supplementary benefit. Deductions are made over the whole period for which loss of earnings is claimed, including the notice period. Earnings and benefits not counted in calculating wages payable in lieu of notice are counted here. Only if the result of calculating overall wages loss is below the amount for wages in lieu of notice is the latter amount paid. This slightly odd position is not always adhered to, although it is not always easy to sort out the facts. For example, in *Hilti (GB) Ltd.* v. *Windridge* [1974] I.C.R.352 unemployment benefit seems only to have been deducted in the period after the expiry of proper notice, but the claimant may have been disqualified for the earlier period. However, the result is logical if the amount of wages in lieu is seen as a minimum rather than as a base. There are difficulties where the employer has actually paid wages in lieu, particularly if the legal entitlement is exceeded. Thus in *Cawthorn & Sinclair Ltd.* v. *Hedger* [1974] I.C.R. 146 the claimant received six months' wages in lieu of notice, but got a new job at a lower wage three weeks later. It was said not to be just and equitable to leave the amount received out of the calculations so that no loss was in fact suffered until the second year after the dismissal. The same rule is applied where the employer pays more than his legal obligation, as in *Hilti* v. *Windridge*. This principle would seem to extend to severance payments by the employer, but presumably only when they are intended to cover future wage loss. For as will be seen below redundancy payments are not to be deducted, so there must be a line between the categories somewhere. The NIRC did not really develop any principle for dealing with collateral benefits beyond retreat into the "just and equitable" formula.

(d) *Loss of protection*
Norton mentioned future loss of protection against

redundancy and unfair dismissal, in the sense that the
claimant must start from scratch again in building up
continuity of employment. To these should be added loss of
entitlement to notice under the Contracts of Employment
Act. This was accepted as a permissible, though speculative,
head of damage in *Hilti* v. *Windridge*, where three weeks'
wages were awarded for loss of a six week notice entitlement.
No doubt more claims under this head will now appear. The
other two categories are more important. Mr. Tewson
received £20 for loss of unfair dismissal protection (less than
one week's wages), but the NIRC said they had no evidence of
local conditions. Obviously the value of protection is lessened
by the likelihood of a fair dismissal or a voluntary quit. So in
Vaughan v. *Weighpack Ltd.* a low figure (£30) was right
because the claimant was unhappy in his job and in poor
health. Amounts awarded have generally been small, whereas
more substantial sums have been awarded for loss of
redundancy protection. Account has to be taken of the
likelihood of future redundancy in the old job. The more
secure it was the less valuable the protection. Similarly, the
security of the new job is relevant. In *Norton* there was no
evidence on either matter, so half the accrued redundancy
entitlement was awarded. This of course is the amount the
employer himself has to pay if he makes a redundancy
payment and it looked as though the NIRC was ensuring that
he could not get away cheaper by dismissing unfairly.
However, it has since been emphasised that each case depends
on the evidence about possible redundancies and the object is
fair compensation (*Bateman* v. *British Leyland U.K. Ltd.*
[1974] I.C.R. 403). Awards of more (*Murphy Telecommuni-
cations* (*Systems*) *Ltd.* v. *Henderson* [1973] I.C.R. 581) and
less (*Vaughan* v. *Weighpack Ltd.*) than half have been made.
Indeed in *York Trailer Ltd.* v. *Sparkes* it was held that
nothing would be allowed for loss of any protection because
the claimant had become self-employed after the dismissal

and so could not be dismissed or become redundant. This is rather dubious as far as loss of redundancy protection goes, for it fails to take account of the loss of benefits if the claimant had remained in the old job. The new occupation should not be looked at exclusively.

One difficulty is where the claimant is unfairly selected for redundancy and the employer has made the statutory payment. In *Yorkshire Engineering Co. Ltd.* v. *Burnham* [1974] I.C.R. 77 it was argued that the amount of the payment should be deducted, following *Stocks* v. *Magna Merchants*. The NIRC held that *Stocks* was wrong even for wrongful dismissal and should not be applied here, and has been followed in *Millington* v. *T.H. Goodwin & Sons* [1975] I.C.R. 104. However, it is clear that no additional sum for loss of redundancy entitlement can be paid: that entitlement has already been cashed in. In *Murphy* v. *Henderson* it was said that the loss could not be attributed to the unfair dismissal, while in *Yorkshire Engineering* it was said, alternatively, that since likelihood of redundancy was 100 per cent. the whole payment has been made for loss of entitlement. It does not matter which approach is taken. The result is the same. The same result will now commonly follow under section 76(3) of the Employment Protection Act, which provides that the amount of the basic award must be deducted from any amount awarded for loss of redundancy entitlement. This will normally leave nothing, except in cases where an employer has a private scheme more generous than the statutory one.

(e) *Loss of pension rights*
This was not raised in *Norton*, but has been important in a number of cases. The fullest discussion is in *Scottish CWS Ltd.* v. *Lloyd* [1973] I.C.R. 137, a decision of the NIRC sitting in Scotland. The claimant is entitled to the return of his own contributions (to which he is usually entitled anyway),

the value of the employer's past contributions and future loss of benefits. The calculation of past contributions gives little problem, although it gives the unfairly dismissed an advantage in that pension schemes generally do not allow the return of employer's contributions, only the freezing of a pension. However, similar awards have been made in, *e.g. Cawthorn & Sinclair.* In *Scottish CWS* no one method of calculating future loss was picked out, although a broad common sense approach was advocated. The NIRC treated the employer's contributions as part of the salary and therefore awarded the annual amount for the estimated period of loss of earnings. There was no superannuation scheme in the new job, but where there are prospects of a pensionable job, as in *Cawthorn & Sinclair*, the amount will be reduced. The court thus attempts to take a realistic view of "total remuneration," and loss of pension benefit may add significantly to the value of awards. These rules have recently been summarised in *Copson & Trahearn* v. *Eversure Accessories Ltd.* [1974] I.R.L.R. 247. For a full discussion, see Jackson.

The relation with most other sources of compensation has been dealt with, except for tax. First, amounts received in tax rebates seem generally to have been disregarded, certainly in calculation of immediate loss of wages, as too insignificant to be calculated (see *Norton*). Nor do they appear in calculations of future wage loss, although their amount might well be quite significant. Now this has been pointed out in a common law decision, employers may argue for deductions. There is nothing to exempt awards from taxation. Presumably they are caught by sections 187-188 of the Income and Corporation Taxes Act 1970, and since the raising of the maximum to £5,200 there is more danger of their going over £5,000 when combined with any other payments.

Redundancy Payments

The ordinary redundancy payment is in the form of a lump sum, but in some circumstances a claimant can secure his weekly remuneration. If an employer fails to consult trade union representatives as required by section 99 of the Employment Protection Act, an IT may make a protective award, requiring the employer to pay the remuneration for the protected period (defined in section 101(5)). The amount of a lump sum redundancy payment is the product of three factors — age, length of service and earnings. For each year of continuous service in the same business during which the claimant was over 40 he receives one and a half week's pay. For each year between 22 and 40 he receives one week's pay. For each year between 18 and 21 he receives half a week's pay. Years are counted back from the date of termination to a maximum of 20. The maximum amount of pay (*i.e.* at date of termination) that can be counted is £80. The maximum payment is thus £2,400 (Redundancy Payments Act, Sched.1 and Calculation of Redundancy Payments Order 1974). The weighting according to age was not at all common in pre-Act schemes, but was introduced, according to Ellis and McCarthy (para. 14), because redundancy was thought to cause sharper anxiety before dismissal and greater difficulty in finding another job and adjusting to a new way of life for older workers. The 20-year limit is arbitrary. No doubt cost had some influence, as had the difficulty in tracing records back before 1945. Again according to Ellis and McCarthy (para. 23) it was thought that over 20 years' service hardship varies little and any extra will be taken care of by the age weighting. But up to 20 years it was thought that increasing length of service indicated greater rights in the job and possibly the need for a greater incentive to move.

The period of continuous employment is determined under Schedule 1 to the Contracts of Employment Act 1972 and has led to some of the most complex decisions under the Act,

particularly where businesses change hands. The full
complexities are discussed in Grunfeld, Chaps. 6 and 7, but
the obscurities of the provisions may easily trap the claimant.
This will be so even though the Employment Protection Act
(Sched. 16, Part II, para. 4) adds to the particulars of terms
of employment which must be included in the written
statement under the Contracts of Employment Act a
statement whether any service with a previous employer
counts as part of continuous employment. The Court of
Appeal seems prepared to hold that employers may be
estopped from denying the correctness of such statements (see
Evenden v. *Guildford City AFC* [1975] I.C.R. 367).
However, the same principle could catch an employee who,
for example, signs a statement that previous service does not
count.

The third element in the calculation, a week's pay, has also
produced complications. Most arise from the fact that the
method of calculation was simply transferred from the
Contracts of Employment Act provisions for guaranteed pay
during notice. These were introduced merely to secure some
kind of minimum pay and are not suitable for the redundancy
payments scheme. For the ordinary situation where there are
normal working hours, pay consists of the number of normal
working hours multiplied by the hourly rate of remuneration.
The problem is what are normal working hours. Overtime is
included only if "the contract fixes the number, or the
minimum number of hours of employment ... and that
number or minimum number of hours exceed the number of
hours without overtime" (Contracts of Employment Act,
Sched.2, para.1(2)). The result, as the courts are constantly
having to tell incensed claimants, is that unless overtime is
obligatory on both employer and employee it does not count.
Even though the claimant may be bound to work a certain
number of hours overtime, only if the employer is bound to
provide that amount of overtime can it be counted. The latest

affirmation of the position by the Court of Appeal is *Tarmac Roadstone Holdings Ltd.* v. *Peacock* [1973] I.C.R. 273. In an industrial relations setting where overtime is worked quite extensively, often as a means of bringing pay up to a reasonable level from the basic rate, failure to take account of overtime working distorts economic realities. It also enhances the attraction of productivity deals guaranteeing higher basic rates. There are also problems because overtime hours are often laid down in local collective agreements, whose effect on the individual contract of employment is far from straightforward, and which are often held not to fix the number of hours contractually (see *e.g. Loman* v. *Merseyside Transport Services Ltd.* [1968] I.T.R 108). Overall, one must agree with Grunfeld (p.233) that the present definition of the normal working week should be scrapped. For those without normal working hours, and shift and rota workers an average is taken of earnings over the previous 12 weeks. This is more straightforward, but if redundancy is in the air such earnings may well be depressed so that even this is not wholly satisfactory. There has been some doubt about what exactly counts as remuneration. *S & U Stores* v. *Wilkes* [1974] I.R.L.R. 283 seems to have settled that sums paid simply by way of reimbursement of expenses do not count. Nor does the value of benefits in kind (*Imperial London Hotels Ltd.* v. *Cooper* [1974] I.R.L.R. 199: free accommodation).

There is no question of abatement because of other earnings or benefits. The factors mentioned are the sole elements in the calculation. The claimant may get a new job within an hour of dismissal, but his payment is unaffected. There are only three situations in which the statutory payment is reduced. First, if a collective agreement's terms are at least as favourable to the claimant as the Act's, then the Secretary of State can make an order of exemption from the Act and only the collectively agreed payments are recoverable (s.11). Secondly, the Redundancy Payments Pension Regulations

1965 allow an employer to reduce or eliminate the statutory payment to a claimant who becomes entitled to an occupational pension on dismissal for redundancy. The pension must be payable immediately and amount annually to at least one-third of 52 weeks' pay, so that the most usual case will be early retirement. The Secretary of State is to decide the meaning of "pension." It may include a lump sum payment, but the return of the claimant's contributions is specifically excluded. The employer may if he chooses make the full statutory payment and claim the rebate: it is for each pension scheme to decide if it is to reduce the statutory entitlement. Thirdly, a job offer from the dismissing employer may destroy the right to a payment. This is discussed in Chapter 6. Redundancy payments are subject to section 187 of the Income and Corporation Taxes Act (see s.412(8)).

It is clear from the disparate purposes of the Redundancy Payments Act and the calculation of payments that they are not intended to provide precise individual compensation. Once it was decided to make the amount of the payment independent of subsequent unemployment, benefits received, etc., it was inevitable that the calculation should be rough and ready. The 1969 Survey does show that in general older, longer service and higher paid claimants, who got larger payments, did suffer more adverse effects (measured largely in terms of financial loss) (Parker and Thomas, pp. 85-88). However, this merely shows that the criteria differentiated roughly according to hardship. It gives no guide to whether compensation overall was too low or too high (see Fryer, p.251). Thus the statement in the introduction to the Survey that the Act "has broadly achieved its social objectives" (para.30) is misleading except in the light of the statement of the objective as to provide "some notional compensation" (para.10). It could hardly fail to do that. But since most of the hardship appears to be financial loss, that could be replaced fairly precisely, it may be that the main reason for having a standard formula was the economic one: all employees should be offered a kind of bonus as an incentive to risk the financial loss and disruption of redundancy. Again, the desire to ensure the acceptance of management decisions on redundancy seems to outweigh the objective of compensation.

Unemployment Benefit

If the claimant has a sufficient contribution record he is entitled to flat-rate benefit, currently £11.10 per week. If the claimant is a married woman, she receives reduced benefit of £7.80 except in rather restricted circumstances. (National Insurance Act 1972, s.1(2), (3), 1975 Act, ss.14(4), (5), 44(2), (3)). He receives an increase of £6.90 for an adult dependant, subject to the conditions of the National Insurance Act 1965, s.43 (1975 Act, s.44). If the dependant is a wife then there is no increase if her earnings from gainful occupation exceed £6.90 per week, nor if they are living apart and the claimant contributes less than £6.90 to maintenance. There is a further increase for each child, so that including Family Allowances the amount is £3.50 for each. The flat-rate of benefit was the "first fundamental principle" of the Beveridge scheme (para.304), following from the more basic assumption that social security meant security up to a minimum. Social insurance was to provide a basic income for subsistence (para.302). Beveridge of course recognised that the normal expenditure of different sections of the community varied greatly, but protection of higher standards was to be for voluntary insurance. This was "an essential part of security; scope and encouragement for it must be provided" (para. 375). This approach is understandable when the major objective is the abolition of the Giant Want, especially in war time with its emphasis on solidarity and equality and a generally low standard of living. These conditions continued some time after the end of World War II, so that the flat-rate principle became enshrined in the National Insurance Act 1946.

It continued to rule unemployment benefit until 1966, when the earnings related benefit scheme was introduced. This was in part a response to the problem of encouraging labour mobility. Higher rates of benefit had been recommended in a NEDC Report in 1963 to ease acceptance of short-term unemployment and reduce the pressure to keep workers on short time. Some see a difference of "social philosophy regarding the practical importance of various concepts of need" (Hauser and Burrows, p.41). The relation of need to prior living standards and commitments was recognised by Beveridge, but by 1966 it was clear that certainly in the unemployment field his hopes that private insurance would be organised had not been fulfilled. The choice was then social insurance or no insurance. Although the shift to low unemployment and rising prosperity may have encouraged the move to protect the differentials of the labour market, the shift of social philosophy is not clear cut.

As it is the labour mobility arguments seem to control many of the scheme's features, in particular its restriction to the short term. Earnings related benefit is payable for only 26 weeks, so it is cut off just when hardship is likely to bite. Nor are benefits paid for the first 12 days of interruption of employment (National Insurance Act 1966, s.2(2)(*c*), 1975 Act, s.14(7)). Here the objective seems to have been to cut costs and to avoid encouraging abuse or malingering. Moreover, the structure of the scheme means that its benefits are not unduly generous. The claimant receives one-third of any earnings between £10 and £30 per week, and 15 per cent. of earnings between £30 and £54 (for 1976: the upper limit is raised each year). This supplement is paid on top of the flat-rate benefit, but the total must not exceed 85 per cent. of the claimant's earnings. This rule is designed to ensure that the claimant does not receive more in benefit than in work after deductions and expenses, unless he is exceptionally low paid. The result is that the low paid benefit least from the supplement, for the flat-rate benefit may easily get near to 85 per cent. of earnings. Earnings are not current earnings, but are based on earnings in the relevant contribution year. The benefit year runs from January to January, and the relevant year is the one in which the period of interruption of employment begins. Benefits governed by that year are determined by earnings in the last complete income tax year (*i.e.* April 6 to April 5). Thus the amount of supplement paid to a claiment becoming unemployed in November 1976 is based on earnings in the tax year April 1974 — April 1975, which are likely to be far below current earnings. Nor does the amount change at the end of the benefit year if the claimant is already receiving a supplement — it is the year in which unemployment begins which matters. The final factor which reduces the effectiveness of the supplement in protecting actual income is the calculation of the weekly earnings figure. This is obtained by dividing total PAYE earnings for the tax year by 50. Any spell of non-payment of wages, *e.g.* during sickness or unemployment, will reduce the figure. For example, if a £1,500 a year man, with a normal weekly figure of £30, is out of work for 10 weeks, his total earnings are reduced to roughly £1,200, and the weekly figure to £24. By contrast, the further a man starts above the upper limit he can afford increasing loss of wages without affecting the supplement. Thus the scheme is not nearly as generous as it appears at first sight. Although it needs considerable overhaul (see further Mesher), it is retained virtually intact in the 1975 Act.

Unemployment benefit is exempt from income tax (Income and Corporation Taxes Act, s.219). In general it is primary, being paid irrespective of means and income from most other sources. Apart from earnings from gainful occupation (discussed in Chap. 3) the only exception is where money is received specifically to replace income lost through unemployment. There have been a number of complications and

amendments to the rule, but the present one was inserted into
the 1967 Regulations by Amendment Regulations in 1971.
Regulation 7(1)(*e*) (1975 Regulations, reg.7(1)(*d*)) now
provides that "a day shall not be treated as a day of
unemployment if it is a day in respect of which a person
receives a payment (whether or not a payment in pursuance of
a legally enforceable obligation) in lieu either of notice or of
the remuneration which he would have received for that day
had his employment not been terminated, so, however, that
the provisions of this subparagraph shall not apply to any day
which does not fall within the period of one year from the
date on which the employment of that person terminated."
Previously the disentitlement where a payment was received
in lieu of remuneration applied only to contracts for a term
certain. There were difficulties in defining this category. The
proviso that legal obligation is unnecessary was introduced
apparently mainly to ensure that Crown servants are covered.
Both these changes have caused problems of interpretation
for the Commissioners, and differences of view. The position
has been resolved by a series of Tribunal decisions, although
the majority opinions differ from the literal interpretation
given to the regulation by the Chief Commissioner in separate
opinions. First a payment is in lieu of remuneration only so
far as it replaces remuneration that would have been received
in the notice period. The claimant in R(U) 7/73 who received
three months' salary, though entitled to one month's notice,
was disentitled only for that month. The proviso on legal
obligation is now held to operate only to ensure that Crown
servants are covered (see also R(U) 8/73). The decision is
based partly on the difficulty of determining for what period
remuneration is replaced once one goes beyond the notice
period. The Chief Commissioner was prepared to face this
difficulty in holding that the regulation applied to any
payment which replaced remuneration, regardless of legal
obligation. He reached that same result in R(U) 7/73 by

holding that the extra payment was in appreciation of past services, rather than in lieu of remuneration. Another reason was that a disentitling provision had to be construed strictly, but this principle is not applied in other contexts. In the converse situation where the claimant receives less than his notice entitlement (C.U. 6/73) he is disentitled for the whole notice period. There is said to be an inevitable inference that the sum received is in satisfaction of all rights under the contract, following R(U) 3/68. The claimant may even be caught if he receives a payment on resignation if it is in return for agreeing to forego his right to notice (R(U) 9/73).

So far as other payments go, it is clear that wrongful dismissal damages are in lieu of remuneration for the notice period (R(U) 3/68). It has been held that since compensation for unfair dismissal contains a similar element it disentitles the claimant for the period of notice (R(U) 5/74). This case is particularly important, for it also holds that the claimant must inform the authorities if he is contemplating making any claim to payment in relation to the termination of his employment. The result appeared at first to be that payment of benefit would be suspended until either the claim was resolved or the notice period expired. However, in C.U. 14/74 it has been held that there ought not to be undue delay in making a decision, although the result of the claim is unknown. Then, inevitably, regulation 7(1)(*e*) cannot be invoked before any payment has been received. If the claimant does not give the information he may be required to repay any benefit received for failing to show due care and diligence in avoiding overpayment, as happened in R(U) 5/74. It presumably does not apply to a claim for a redundancy payment, which will not be regarded as replacing remuneration. If an IT recommends re-engagement with full pay made up for the interval, the claimant is disentitled for the whole period (C.U. 17/73). In this case repayment of benefit was not required. When section 112 of the

Employment Protection Act, allowing recoupment by the government of unemployment benefit from employers making payments, is implemented, repayment by the claimant of any sum recouped will not be allowed (s.112(5)). Further, section 113 confirms the result of C.U. 17/73 and provides that claimants subject to an order for continuation of a contract of employment under section 78 or to a protective award under section 101 shall be treated as employed. Such payments, including elements of unfair dismissal compensation that replace remuneration, now disentitle claimants under regulation 7(1)(*l*) of the 1975 Regulations, inserted by the 1976 Amendment Regulations.

Supplementary Benefit

The aim of supplementary benefit is to provide no more than a minimum income. Therefore, it will only bring the claimant's income up to a fixed level, regardless of former earnings. In the language of the Supplementary Benefit Act, the amount of benefit is the amount by which the claimant's resources fall short of his requirements (Sched.2, para.1). Thus the definition of the claimant's requirements sets the level to which his income will be raised.

Requirements

There is a basic scale, regarded by the SBC as covering "all normal needs which can be foreseen, including food, fuel and light, the normal repair and replacement of clothing, household sundries (but not major items of bedding and furnishing) and provision for such amenities as newspapers, entertainments and television licences" (SB Handbook, para.44). The requirements and resources of a husband and wife living together (or cohabitors) are added together, as can be those of any other person for whose requirements the householder has to provide (Sched.2, para.3). The SBC seems to regard all the claimant's children under 16 in the household as in this category, in which case there must be aggregation. However, the opinion of the Court of Appeal in *K.* v. *JMP Co. Ltd.* [1975] 1 All E.R. 1030 was that if the child had independent resources to cover the necessities of life then it fell outside paragraph 3. Generally, the SBC includes children over 16 only if they are at school or are low-paid apprentices (Handbook, para.13). If there is aggregation only the householder can claim for them all. The current scale provides £17.75 for a husband and wife living together, £10.90 for a single householder, plus an allowance for others ranging from £3.10 for a child under five to £8.70 for a person over 18. There are slightly higher rates for the blind and also a long-term scale which is only applicable to pensioners and those on supplementary benefit, without being required to register for work, for at least two years. The unemployed are thus restricted to the basic scale.

To this is added the net rent paid by the householder. The rules here are very complex, so what follows is no more than a brief summary. "Householder" is not defined and the Court of Appeal in *R.* v. *Sheffield Supplementary Benefits Appeal Tribunal, ex parte Shine* [1975] 1 W.L.R. 624 refused to apply a strict legal definition. The SBC takes it to mean the person who is the owner of the home or is responsible for rent. Clearly there are many non-dependants who live in another's household with an independent claim to benefit. Here there are two categories. One is where an inclusive charge for board and lodging is paid. Here paragraph 17 simply says that requirements are to be the appropriate amount not below the scale rate. The SBC will generally pay the board and lodging charge, providing it is reasonable, plus an allowance for clothes and personal expenses (for many elements of the scale rate are included in the board and lodging charge). This allowance is currently £3.50 for a single person (£3.80 for a couple). The other category is a non-householder, who receives the appropriate scale rate plus £1. The distinction between these categories is a difficult and frequently contested one, particularly where the SBC finds lodging arrangements not to be "on a commercial basis" (para.116), so that the claimant is defined as a non-householder.

The net rent is not necessarily what is paid to a landlord. On the plus side are many outgoings, such as rates and allowances for repairs and insurance (para.13(3)(*b*)). On the minus side, proceeds from sub-letting have to be deducted, and the SBC also deducts any amount in the rent that is to cover heating and lighting, which is taken to be covered by the scale rate. The deduction is either the actual amount if calculable or certain standard amounts (*e.g.* £1.20 per week for heating). The SBC may also refuse to pay unreasonable rent (para.13(1)(*a*)), either because the accommodation is not reasonable for the claimant, or because the rent is not reasonable for the accommodation. The standards applied to the first issue are slightly vague. A claimant is not expected to lower his standard of accommodation, unless it is private property which is excessively large or luxurious or is in an unduly expensive neighbourhood. In these cases the rent will be met in full for a short period only, except in very exceptional circumstances. The SBC will inform the claimant how long he has before the amount is reduced to a reasonable rent (see SBC Notes and News No.3, where new guidelines, superceding those in the Handbook, are set out). The old maximum rent level for particular areas seems to have been abandoned.

Rent will normally be regarded as reasonable for the accommodation if it is for local authority or housing association property or is controlled or registered. Otherwise, the estimated fair rent is taken, in the light of information from the local authority and the rent officer. In particular, if the local authority would accept the rent as reasonable for rent allowance purposes, then the SBC will normally accept it and that the claimant is not over-housed. More than the estimated fair rent may be paid if, considering all the claimant's circumstances and the availability of cheaper accommodation, the SBC decides that the claimant has little alternative to staying where he is. The SBC must meet amounts of mortgage interest for owner-occupiers, although there is no specific power to meet capital repayments (para.13(3)(*b*)). This may cause hardship, but building societies may accept payments of interest only and the SBC may allow the amount of capital repayments to be offset against some sources of income (most usefully, income from sub-letting) in calculating resources. The new guidelines state that the question whether the outgoings (including a repairs and insurance allowance, rates etc.) are unreasonable will be decided in relation to the claimant's resources at the time when the commitment was taken on. Thus most owner-occupiers will get their full mortgage interest, but there is still the possibility that the SBC may decide that the claimant is over-housed. Here it seems that the claimant will have to argue that the difficulty and expense of moving amount to very exceptional circumstances if the full amount is to be met for long. This seems at odds with the rest of the SBC's new policy.

It is fortunately no longer necessary to discuss the wage-stop. This rule, which limited the amount of benefit to what the claimant would receive in his normal full-time employment, was abolished by section 19 of the Child Benefit Act 1975.

Resources

Since supplementary benefit is supposed to be a residual programme, merely a safety-net to catch those who slip through the National Insurance system, the general rule is that all other sources of income must count in computing a claimant's resources. Family allowances, the main National Insurance benefits and maintenance payments count in full (Supplementary Benefits Act 1966, Sched.2, para.24). The first £4 of earnings (£2 if required to register for work) is now disregarded (*ibid*. para.23), as is £4 of other income. All kinds of income come under this heading, including regular payments from relatives, charities, etc. and potential tax refunds to strikers (para.25A, added in 1971). No more than £1 of pensions or periodical redundancy payments may be disregarded under this head (para.25). The only resources specifically excluded are death and maternity grants, gallantry awards, the earnings of a child or a person in full-time secondary education, the value of owner-occupied property and the first £1200 of capital. The SBC in its discretion (given by para.26) disregards the value of personal possessions, payments from relatives etc. for items not covered by the scale rate and occasional gifts. The value of these disregards, even after recent increases, is still very low compared with the amounts set in 1948 (first 10s. of earnings for an unemployed man), and even more so compared with those of 1935. Certainly claimants are treated less favourably than unemployment benefit claimants, who can earn £4.50 a week without losing their right to benefit. Such discrimination might have been justified if supplementary benefit now remained the minor part of the social security system that Beveridge intended. But National Insurance has not attained his principles of adequacy and comprehensiveness so that supplementary benefit with its higher rates has remained an important part of the system. In June 1973 when 40.4 per cent. of registered unemployed men were receiving unemployment benefit, 49.2 per cent. were receiving supplementary benefit, mostly not in conjunction with unemployment benefit because eligibility was exhausted (D.E. Gazette, March 1974, p.216). In such a situation it is much harder to justify many of the restrictive supplementary benefit rules and the maintenance of dual standards.

Capital is treated in this way. Any income it actually produces is ignored. Then it is assumed to produce 25p a week income, to be counted in full, for each complete £50 over

£1,200 (para.22). This is more than anyone could expect actually to receive in interest. The justification is that "a person with appreciable capital must be expected to spend some of this on day-to-day living expenses. As the person's capital falls, the amount of supplementary benefit will increase" (Handbook, para.31). In a means-tested scheme the pressure for such a rule is strong, but there is counter-pressure in the argument that it penalises those who have tried to make provision against misfortune in contrast to those who have spent instead of saved. The value of personal possessions is ignored totally, and the contrast with capital is sharp. It may be, however, that the recent increase in the disregard (formerly capital over £300 was regarding as producing the notional income) has provided a rough compromise.

The distinction between capital and income is an important one, for it is usually advantageous to the claimant to have a sum treated as capital. Redundancy payments in a lump sum and tax refunds (except to strikers) are treated as capital. The SBC will treat a payment by the employer of the last week's wages as income for the period until the next normal pay-day. This means that usually an unemployed man will not be able to claim full supplementary benefit for the first week (or month if monthly paid) of unemployment, in contrast to the unemployment benefit position. Policy is less clear about other payments from an employer like holiday pay, wages in lieu of notice, damages and the loss of wages element of unfair dismissal compensation. The SBC apparently (see Lynes, p.70) treats the first two as income, to cover the number of pay periods they represent, although this may be reversed on appeal. Since the last two are usually not paid until some weeks after employment has terminated these are normally treated as capital even though they both contain sums to cover lost wages. The decision of the Divisional Court in *R. v. West London Supplementary Benefits Appeal*

Tribunal, ex parte Taylor [1975] 1 W.L.R. 1048 confirms that
the court will only interfere with a categorisation if no
tribunal properly directing itself would come to the conclusion which is challenged, so that the SBC has a good deal of
freedom. The other point of the *Taylor* case, that arrears of
maintenance payments cannot, if treated as income, be
regarded as income for future weeks, does not seem to help in
the unemployment context. Once again there is a clear
contrast with the unemployment benefit rules, where capital
is ignored, and only specified payments disentitle the
claimant.

Chapter 6

NEGLECT OF JOB OPPORTUNITIES

All the schemes contain sanctions against those who neglect job opportunities. This is not surprising, given the concern about work-shy claimants, but the breadth of the provisions and the discretion they allow are noteworthy. Further, interesting differences in the interpretation of very similar rules can be discerned.

Wrongful Dismissal

Anyone claiming damages has a duty to take reasonable steps to mitigate his loss. He must take reasonable action to find a new job and accept reasonable offers. It is for the employer to prove breach of this duty. Obviously, this "cannot be a question of law, but must be one of fact in the circumstances of each case" (Bankes L.J. in *Payzu Ltd.* v. *Saunders* [1919] 1 K.B. 581 at p.588). However, certain factors that are generally relevant can be picked out.

If a job offer comes from the defendant employer, the state of relations between the parties should be taken into account. In *Shindler* v. *Northern Raincoat Co. Ltd.* [1960] 1 W.L.R. 1038 the claimant alleged that offers were made purely as an attempt to reduce the amount of damages. Diplock J. rejected that view, but clearly the litigation and rows with the claimant were relevant to the decision that refusal of the offer was reasonable. There is a good deal of flexibility about salary rates. The claimant in *Yetton* v. *Eastwoods Froy Ltd.* [1967] 1

W.L.R. 104 had been employed at £7,500, yet it was held reasonable for him to apply only for jobs in the £8,000 to £10,000 range, being prepared to accept £7,500 and coming down to £5,000 after six months. Perhaps the more important issue in the case was that, having been managing director, he was not unreasonable in refusing an offer of a job as a joint assistant managing director in view of the loss of status involved. A similar approach was taken to blue collar employment in *Edwards* v. *SOGAT* [1971] Ch.354, a case of expulsion from a union. The Court of Appeal found that a skilled man was entitled to refuse to do labouring work. It seems that the claimant is expected to lower his sights as the length of unemployment increases. However, no hard guidelines can be laid down when so many personal factors are relevant and quite a wide range of conduct can be described as reasonable.

One problem is where there are negotiations for reinstatement and the claimant is advised not to accept other jobs. If the negotiations fail then it is not clear what weight the courts would give to the hope of recovering the old job.

Unfair Dismissal

The common law duty of mitigation is incorporated into the calculation of the compensatory award by section 76(4) of the Employment Protection Act 1975. However, the *Tewson* rule is that the irreducible minimum of the amount of wages for the notice period is not subject to any deductions. The duty to mitigate can only affect overall loss of wages. Since often the bulk of this will occur after the IT decision, few cases have raised mitigation problems. *A.G. Bracey Ltd.* v. *Iles* [1973] I.R.L.R. 210 confirms that the claimant does not have to take the first job that comes along when it would be more reasonable to wait for a better job and reduce the overall loss.

A further sanction is that if the claimant unreasonably prevents an order for reinstatement or re-engagement from taking effect, then the IT must take that into account as a failure to mitigate loss (s.72(6)).

Redundancy Payments

Since the length of unemployment has no bearing on a redundancy payment, there is no duty to seek a new job. Indeed, one of the purposes of the Redundancy Payments Act was to allow the claimant more time to find the right job, although it is disputed whether it has any effect on length of unemployment (see Fryer, pp.251-252). However, in some circumstances refusal of the offer of a job by the dismissing employer will deprive the claimant of a payment. These are set out in section 2 of the Act, as amended by Schedule 16, Part I, para.2 to the Employment Protection Act 1975. The contract offered must be to take effect within four weeks of the ending of the old employment, and can be of renewal of the existing contract or re-engagement under a new one. It must either be on the same terms and conditions as the existing contract, or, if the terms differ, constitute suitable employment in relation to the claimant. Then if the claimant unreasonably refuses the offer he loses his right to a payment. There are only minor changes from the old law. There is no longer any requirement that an offer of different terms be in writing, nor need identical employment start immediately on the termination of the existing employment. Thus most of the decisions on the old section 2 are still relevant.

In view of the presumption of redundancy it is for the employer to prove that the offer has been made (*Simpson* v. *Dickinson* [1972] I.C.R. 474). It seems to follow that, although in *McCreadie* v. *Thomson & MacIntyre Ltd.* [1971] 1 W.L.R. 1193 the House of Lords held that a notice posted in the works constituted a sufficient offer, it is necessary that the individual claimant in fact reads or receives the offer.

The major decisions are on whether the employment is suitable or a refusal reasonable. It may be that logically these two questions should be separated, as the Court of Session thought in *Carron Co.* v. *Robertson* [1967] I.T.R. 484, but in practice ITs appear to allow them to overlap since suitability must be assessed in relation to the particular claimant. This is not regarded as an error of law justifying interference providing all the relevant factors are considered. ITs thus have a good deal of freedom in deciding questions of fact and the courts are reluctant to alter their findings. Lord Parker C.J. has said that "suitability means employment which is substantially equivalent to the employment which has ceased ..." (*Taylor* v. *Kent C.C.* [1969] 2 Q.B. 560 at p.566), but later cases have retreated from attempts to provide general definitions (see *Collier* v. *Smith's Dock Ltd.* [1969] I.T.R. 338). Now, providing the IT takes into account loss of status as well as loss of pay or other matters it will not be regarded as misdirecting itself. In *Taylor's* case a job in a pool of replacement teachers was not suitable for an ex-headmaster, though his salary would be the same. Similarly, *Harris* v. *Turner & Sons* [1973] I.C.R. 31 emphasises that status is relevant in considering manual workers, although as *Collier's* case and *Kane* v. *Raine & Co. Ltd.* [1974] I.C.R. 300 show, ITs are free to decide that a small loss of status does not affect suitability. In contrast, the NIRC held in *Morganite Crucible Ltd.* v. *Street* [1972] I.C.R. 110 that the anticipated length of the new job is generally irrelevant, provided that it is regular, rather than merely temporary employment. More personal matters such as domestic circumstances, health etc. are often treated as affecting the reasonableness of refusal, but many touch both questions, *e.g.* an increase in travelling time. Here there is even less legal control, so that the IT has almost complete discretion.

These rules do not fit easily with the idea that making a payment will smooth the acceptance of redundancy or with the general irrelevance of employment prospects following dismissal. But if redundancy is narrowly defined as surplus labour, then it can be said there was no "real" redundancy if a suitable job was available. The result is that the worker has a big incentive to accept internal re-arrangements of work and that management control of the redundancy situation is reinforced. This is especially the case when the courts have allowed so much flexibility in the definition of suitability, with the danger that employers might make offers simply as an attempt to avoid making a payment. It is hard to see why refusal of a job with the old employer is relevant, while refusal of any others is not, but if the illogical rule must be retained then suitability should be more tightly defined.

Unemployment Benefit

The National Insurance Act 1965 contains another complex provision in section 22(2)(*b*) to (*e*) (Social Security Act 1975, s.20(1)(*b*) to (*e*)), where the various situations in which neglect of job opportunities may lead to disqualification are detailed. All the subsections are variations on (*b*): "after a situation in any suitable employment has been notified to him by an employment exchange or other recognised agency, or by or on behalf of an employer, as vacant, or about to become vacant, he has without good cause refused or failed to apply for that situation or refused to accept that situation when offered to him." Paragraphs (*d*) and (*e*) deal with failure to follow recommendations or accept training opportunities. Only paragraph (*c*) does not contain the good cause exception, but since that requires neglect of a reasonable opportunity of suitable employment, usually the same issues will be relevant (see R(U) 5/71). Then section 22(5) (s.20(4)) provides some definition of suitability:

"For the purposes of this section, employment shall not be deemed to be employment suitable in the case of any person if it is either —
(*a*) employment in a situation vacant in consequence of a

stoppage of work due to a trade dispute; or

(*b*) employment in his usual occupation in the district where he was last ordinarily employed at a rate of remuneration lower, or on conditions less favourable, than those which he might reasonably have expected to obtain having regard to those which he habitually obtained in his usual occupation in that district, or would have obtained if he had continued to be so employed; or

(*c*) employment in his usual occupation in any other district at a rate of remuneration lower, or on conditions less favourable, than those generally observed in that district by agreement between associations of employers and employees, or, failing any such agreement, than those generally recognised in that district by good employers;

but, after the lapse of such an interval from the date on which he became unemployed as in the circumstances of the case is reasonable, employment shall not be deemed to be unsuitable by reason only that it is employment of a kind other than employment in his usual occupation if it is employment at a rate of remuneration not lower, and on conditions not less favourable than those generally observed by agreement between associations of employers and of employees or, failing such agreement, than those generally recognised by good employers."

The first issue is the relation of the disqualification with the availability condition. If the claimant puts restrictions on the employment he is willing to accept he is only unavailable if consequently he has no reasonable prospects of employment. Thus an offer outside those restrictions may still be suitable, although if it goes outside to a material degree it will be unsuitable (R(U) 2/59). Secondly, the deeming provisions need some explanation. Provision (*a*) is straightforward.

Provisions (*b*) and (*c*) only apply if the offer is in the claimant's usual occupation. Then if the conditions are fulfilled it is forbidden to hold the job suitable whatever the merits. The standard is what is normal in the district, not the claimant's last job. So in R(U) 9/64 a job without tea breaks could not be deemed unsuitable because it was common for smaller firms in the district not to provide them, despite the fact that this was contrary to union policy. If the conditions are not fulfilled, then the matter must be decided on the merits. There is no presumption that jobs outside the conditions are suitable. Similarly, the concluding words of the subsection forbid a finding of unsuitability if the conditions are fulfilled, but there is no presumption of unsuitability if they are not. This is explained in R(U) 5/68, where it was stressed that the concluding words apply only where the *only* reason for unsuitability is that the job is outside the claimant's usual occupation.

A claimant may be said to have been unemployed so long or his personal circumstances changed so much that he no longer has a usual occupation. In this case section 22(5) does not apply at all. In R(U) 15/62 the claimant was a builder's labourer who developed a cardiac disability. After five years' unemployment he was offered sheltered and low-paid employment as a Remploy trainee. He refused the job and was disqualified. His usual occupation could not be taken as one he was incapable of doing, so there was no deeming. All the circumstances had to be considered, including physical and mental capabilities, the nature and accessibility of work, earnings and the length of unemployment. This case also illustrates one of the few rules on the definition of suitability, that the fact that the claimant will be worse off financially in the job than he is on benefit or was in his last job is not in itself relevant. The claimant had written "Give me a job where I can live and not starve and I will do it," yet the Commissioner was bound to follow the Tribunal decision

R(U) 10/61. The level of earnings can count as one factor in the decision, but it seems unrealistic to prevent the authorities from finding that a claimant should not be forced to lower his income.

This strictness contrasts with the more flexible approach to more subjective reasons for refusing a job, generally considered under the just cause head. Matters of conscience are usually relevant, notably religious objections to working on Sundays or Saturdays. These have been stretched to include the objection of a vegetarian to working as a secretary in a sausage and pie makers (C.U. 14/68), but it seems the ground must be generally recognised as one of principle. So the claimant who would not work in an Ordnance factory because she thought (wrongly) it was specially dangerous was disqualified (R(U) 32/56). Her belief was genuine, but the test was not completely subjective. Similarly, domestic responsibilities are taken into account, but only up to a point. The claimant in R(U) 20/60 was entitled to refuse a job starting earlier than anyone could arrive to look after her baby, but it was said that a married woman must be prepared to rearrange her domestic affairs within reasonable limits, *e.g.* giving up cooking meals for a grown-up family. And the longer unemployment lasts, the more flexibility is required. If a claimant has no domestic responsibilities the range of suitable employment is very wide. In R(U) 34/58 an unmarried labourer aged 22 unemployed for seven months with no prospects of local work in the Shetland Islands was disqualified for turning down a job 750 miles away in Bletchley.

Supplementary Benefit

If the claimant is (or would be) disqualified for unemployment benefit, then the deduction of 40 per cent. of the single person's scale rate applies with the usual exceptions. But the

SBC invokes a much wider range of powers to deal with the voluntarily unemployed. In particular, if it is known that a particular suitable job is available to the claimant, who would be disqualified for unemployment benefit, supplementary benefit may be summarily stopped or refused. This action may also be taken following repeated incidents of voluntary unemployment in an area where jobs are abundant, if the claimant suffers from no disability and there are no children, or other dependants who might suffer hardship (Handbook, para.202). Fisher (para.259) says that repeated here means at least three incidents in the past six months. Nonetheless, this harsh sanction affected 15,000 claimants in 1971 (Fisher, para.233). The SBC derives its authority from its general power contained in the Supplementary Benefit Act, Sched.2, para.4(1) to reduce or withhold benefit in exceptional circumstances. Fisher (para.257) doubted that these circumstances were truly exceptional, and considered that more precise definition of criteria was needed. It is hard to justify going beyond the unemployment benefit test, which requires refusal of a specific opportunity, and even then a complete withdrawal of benefit takes on a penal aspect. It is arguable that since section 12 of the Act provides a special procedure for sending a claimant who is neglecting to maintain himself or his dependants to a re-establishment centre, subject to a prior decision by an Appeal Tribunal, the SBC does not have the power to evade this procedure. However, since there are few centres there must be some lesser sanction than prosecution under section 30 for neglect to maintain. Thus the SBC continues to rely on paragraph 4(1), but it is hoped that it will be used in truly exceptional cases only, and that the routine controls described below will be tried first. The danger is in the freedom given to individual officials, when an appeal may not be heard until several weeks with only "urgent need" payments have passed.

A more common procedure is to call claimants for a special

interview, usually with a specialist unemployment review officer (URO). Roughly 40 per cent. of those called for interview appear to stop claiming benefit shortly before or after the interview. Anybody can be interviewed if it is thought that he needs help in solving a special difficulty, but Fisher (para.275) lists a number of situations in which a claimant will be interviewed. This include (a) where the claimant appears to be persistently unemployed without good cause (persistent includes two instances of *e.g.* misconduct, within a year); (b) a change to casual work; (c) a year's unemployment after a previous review; (d) the possibility of action under sections 12 or 30. The Handbook (para.205) suggests that except in the cases of persistent voluntary unemployment this procedure will not be applied to those within five years of retirement age. The URO has to decide why the claimant is not in work and provide continued benefit, help, advice, persuasion, reduction or withdrawal of benefit, or prosecution, as the situation demands. Fisher recognised the possible conflicts in such a wide range of functions, but considered that the UROs were valuable both in discouraging voluntary unemployment and in their "welfare" role. However, they point out that the second role is particularly necessary when unemployment is high and that a public image of the officers as hostile will detract from this. It would be desirable if there was a special interview before benefit was reduced or withdrawn under paragraph 4(1)(*b*).

The other control procedure mentioned in the Handbook is the making of awards for limited periods, usually known as the "four week rule." This procedure, currently suspended, has recently been amended. Now instead of benefit terminating automatically at the end of the four weeks the claimant is called for interview with the URO. However, the conditions for application of the procedure remain much the same. It is applied to single unskilled men under 45 in areas with good opportunities for unskilled work. They are told that they ought to be able to get a job within four weeks and that benefit may be withdrawn unless they show good reason for still being unemployed. In particular, consideration will be given to any handicap which the claimant has in finding work (Handbook, para.203). Other claimants under 45 in the same areas may be interviewed after three months. Claimants over 45 used to be interviewed after six months, but it is not known whether this continues.

The amendments to the rule remove some of the legal objections to it, notably the apparent decision about eligibility four weeks in advance, when sufficient evidence could not be available. However, many of the more practical problems pointed to by critics remain. These are fully described by Meacher in her study of the old rule. The rule is sometimes applied in areas where it is questionable whether good job opportunities do exist, despite the advice from the Employment Services Agency (Handbook, para.203), and it is also said that many skilled men are treated as unskilled. Moreover, new problems are created. Application of the rule is no longer limited to fit claimants. Those who are incapable of work are not required to register for work, but there remains a large number of physically and mentally handicapped claimants. Their difficulties should of course emerge at the interview, but the danger is that they may suffer hardship through withdrawal of benefit if they fail to attend an interview which can sound intimidating. Moreover, given the ambivalent position which the URO is in, it requires particular sensitivity to ensure that the claimant's full personal circumstances emerge. Since the result of the changes in the rule will be for more interviews to take place (if there are areas with good opportunities for unskilled work!), it may be questioned whether the staff will be able to achieve this sensitivity.

The URO also has enormous discretion in deciding whether the claimant has shown a good reason for remaining unemployed, although it is not known what standards he may be instructed to apply by the A Code. Thus it is not surprising that harsh decisions are sometimes made. The URO is being asked to hold the balance between protection of the public purse and alleviation of hardship when the legislature refuses to say where the proper balance is. The Fisher Committee (para.267) considered that somewhat harder criteria should be provided, so that in general the claimant must have had a specific job notified to him before benefit is withdrawn. A rule of this sort, retaining the freedom to deal with the claimant who is discouraging offers, would be desirable. Once again, it is hard to justify going beyond the unemployment benefit rules on neglect of job opportunities and availability for work.

Chapter 7

CONCLUSION

The first impression gained from this survey of the rules
governing compensation for unemployment is probably of a
fragmented, uncoordinated mass that it would be misleading
to call a system. Even when the main sources of compensation
were damages for wrongful dismissal and social security
benefits, the common law had considerable problems in
accommodating the tax system and social security benefits.
The *Gourley* rule represents a rough compromise on tax, but
the rules on deductibility of social security benefits from
common law damages are hopelessly confused. The addition
of new statutory benefits in the forms of redundancy
payments and compensation for unfair dismissal have further
complicated the issues. Thus redundancy payments have
wrongly been deducted from damages, while from the social
security point of view there are difficult problems about when
receipt of these payments should disqualify the claimant for
benefit. Nor have the courts fully resolved the relation of
other benefits to compensation for unfair dismissal.

Naturally, it is too much to expect a perfectly interlocking
structure, when different benefits have different objectives.
Moreover, there is an inherent difficulty in trying to
accommodate lump sum payments with periodic payments
that probably cannot be overcome. Nevertheless, a good deal
could be done to rationalise the law. Some legislation is
necessary to untangle the law on deductions from common

law damages. The opportunity should be taken to separate the rules for wrongful dismissal from those for calculating damages in tort. Although the common law action is losing importance in the face of the unfair dismissal legislation, it does still act as a deterrent to the employer. It would be wrong if the employer was able to break his contract with impunity by claiming to deduct a large assortment of benefits from the damages he would otherwise pay. A similar principle was recognised by the NIRC in setting the minimum compensation for unfair dismissal as the amount of wages that would have been paid in lieu of notice. To extend such a rule to all wrongful dismissals might be going too far, but certainly unemployment benefit and redundancy payments should not be deducted. The doctrine of mitigation of damages might remain. This could be done if jurisdiction over wrongful dismissal is transferred to the ITs. Some change may also be necessary in the rules for unfair dismissal, especially since receipt of compensation will result in disentitlement for unemployment benefit during the notice period. Regulations under section 112 of the Employment Protection Act should remove some of these problems.

Apart from the lack of co-ordination among benefits, there is also an inevitable fragmentation in the purpose of benefits, the qualifications for them and the way in which they are used to encourage certain sorts of behaviour. The most generous benefits generally have the narrowest qualifying conditions. Thus redundancy payments and unfair dismissal compensation which attempt to compensate for loss of the job as well as simple loss of income, require some period of connection with a particular job. These requirements are being reduced in the unfair dismissal context, but the contrast remains with unemployment benefit where some connection is required with the labour market in general, and supplementary benefits where no past connection with employment is necessary. Similarly, the new benefits require either a termination or a repudiation by the employer. It is true, of course, that claimants who leave their jobs voluntarily without just cause are disqualified for unemployment benefit, which amounts to much the same thing. However, the disqualification lasts only for six weeks and the claimant is eligible for a reduced rate of supplementary benefit.

Here the paradox of the welfare state first appears. The more benefits the state provides, the more means it has for controlling behaviour through the threat of withdrawal of benefit. And the larger the benefit, the greater the sanction. To this extent, in its qualifying conditions, the social security system appears to contain less disincentives to voluntary unemployment. However, this may not be the practical effect. Those with most to lose in terms of redundancy payments or compensation for unfair dismissal are most likely to receive *e.g.* golden handshakes or pension benefits. Moreover, there is the social security system to fall back on. Thus, as always, disqualification falls hardest on the claimant with few other resources, while denial of social security benefits usually leaves the claimant with nowhere else to go.

This situation certainly affects the rules for selecting claimants according to the reason for dismissal, where the approach to misconduct is roughly uniform in the formal sense. The precise definition of redundancy has little to do with hardship or the claimant's merits, but is dictated more by the economic need to encourage labour mobility. This may be why the amounts of redundancy payments have remained relatively low, compared to the limits introduced for compensation for unfair dismissal. Legislation here was more concerned to pick out a deserving class of claimants, but one not based on need as such. These definitions contain their exclusion of those guilty of misconduct although a much wider class is excluded, *e.g.* those dismissed for lack of capability. By contrast the older common law and social security systems generally restrict exclusion to misconduct, although this may have a slightly wider meaning than in unfair dismissal. However, it may be that its interpretation for unemployment benefit purposes will be influenced by the unfair dismissal legislation. Here, the possibility of disqualification is probably as well known to workers as the possibility of loss of other rights.

The social security system offers further potent incentives in the way its benefits are calculated. This appeared in its starkest form in the wage stop. This was said not to be intended as an incentive to the claimant to find work, but must have acted as a powerful inducement for low-wage workers to stay in employment. The rule that an earnings related supplement must not take unemployment benefit over 85 per cent. of the claimant's (out-of-date) earnings has a similar effect, though not so well known. It is often argued that the provision of earnings-related benefits encourages claimants to remain unemployed longer and be more selective about the jobs they will take. Indeed this was part of the reason for introducing these benefits, so may be a good thing. The evidence of the Daniel survey (pp.123-131) is that the amount of weekly benefit had little effect on intensity of job-seeking, although it did affect the minimum wage the claimant was prepared to accept. Overall, Daniel's conclusion is that the level of benefits is not high enough to discourage claimants from working and that it is the physical, social and psychological characteristics of claimants that mainly determine keenness to work (p.151).

In provisions aimed at ensuring that claimants do not neglect opportunities of work, the social security system becomes more powerful. It seems that once the other three sources of compensation have selected their deserving claimants they are treated rather gently. The duty to mitigate loss is a flexible and undemanding one. By contrast, the social security system, having allowed a much wider class to benefit, imposes a further selection here. The unemployment benefit claimant must show that he is available for work, is not placing unreasonable restrictions on the type of work he will accept and is also liable to be disqualified for neglect of job opportunities. He will probably be required to widen the class of jobs he will accept sooner than the doctrine of mitigation would require. The supplementary benefit claimant is subject to a wider range of measures, including the possibilities of benefit being cut off completely and of prosecution. He is also subject to a much less controlled discretion in the hands of officials about the kind of work he ought to accept. Here, where the pressure is aimed directly at the claimant's behaviour, it is at its most intense. It bears most, as always, on those with few other resources to fall back on.

It is at least clear that all the main compensation schemes exhibit concern to discourage voluntary idleness. In the more generous schemes this is done mainly by carefully defining the class to benefit. What pressure is in fact exerted through employees' concern to avoid losing these potential benefits is unknown. Clearly the fact that the social security system exists with its much wider coverage removes some of the sting. However, the social security system applies its own sanctions, which are the more stringent because the majority of its claimants will have no or little other form of compensation for their unemployment.

Apart from these general pressures towards work the system also works to reinforce management control and discipline. The obligations implied into contracts give the employer considerable freedom: the employee must obey his lawful orders and there is some doubt about the scope of legality here. Further, express contractual terms override any implied rights and obligations. Statute has provided minimum periods of notice, but in general freedom of contract is unchecked. This naturally tends to the advantage of the more powerful party to the contract, *i.e.* usually the employer, who tends to lay down the rules. Thus a standard form of contract for executives which I have seen can still provide for summary dismissal for any act of disobedience. The courts in the redundancy context, by allowing a subjective test of the employer's reason for dismissal, have further reinforced this trend. However, in considering the unfairness of dismissal the courts have broken free from relying on the express contract to consider the reasonableness of the employer's conduct. Traditionally the unemployment benefit authorities had followed the common law approach and gone further in providing sanctions behind management's control over discipline in the workplace and conduct outside it. There is now evidence that the authorities are being influenced by the new standards of "industrial morality" developed in the unfair dismissal context. The strictness of the law here may therefore be in the process of relaxation. Even so, employees still know that breaches of discipline may well result in loss of many benefits.

Readers can no doubt find many other considerations in the rules governing compensation for unemployment beyond pure compensation for hardship. It is inevitable that any such system will contain similar elements of social control. Most readers will probably conclude that it is useful and necessary to discourage "scrounging" and idleness. However, they should still ask whether the rules presently reflect the right balance between compensation and control. Given the considerable powers that do exist, they should also ask if further measures to control "scrounging" are necessary. The pressure for further control will probably always be here. The work ethic is strong even in times of high unemployment. Thus the Fisher Committee (para.243) were adamant that it was right to continue to put pressure on claimants to work even when this resulted in someone willing to work being unable to find a job. Finally they should compare the pressures put on the poorer claimant, who may have little alternative source of income to social security benefits, with those imposed on other unemployed people, who may have golden handshakes, tax rebates for several months and other sources of income that tend to be more available the better-off one is. Perhaps one of the main effects of the system is to reinforce the inequalities of work and help retain a pool of low-wage labour.

REFERENCES

Altman: R. Altman, *Availability for Work : A Study in Unemployment Compensation* (1950).

Asia: B.S. Asia, "Employment Relation : Common Law Concept and Legislative Definition," 55 Yale L.J. 76 (1945).

Beveridge: Social Insurance and Allied Services, Report by Sir W. Beveridge, Cmd. 6404 (1942).

Brittain: J.A. Brittain, "The Incidence of Social Security Payroll Taxes," 61 Am. Econ. R. 110 (1971).

Cooper: K.D. Cooper, "A Collateral Benefits Principle," 49 Can. Bar Rev. 501 (1971).

Daniel: W.W. Daniel, *A National Survey of Unemployment* (1974).

D.E. Gazette, March 1974: Characteristics of the Unemployed : Sample Survey June 1973, *Department of Employment Gazette*, March 1974, 211.

D.E. Gazette, Sept. 1974: *Department of Employment Gazette*, Sept. 1974.

Donovan: Report of the Royal Commission on Trade Unions and Employers' Associations, 1965-1968, Cmnd. 3623.

Ellis and McCarthy: N.D. Ellis and W.E.J. McCarthy, *Introduction and Interpretation, in Effects of the Redundancy Payments Act*, Social Survey Division of Office of Population Censuses and Surveys (1971).

Fisher: Report of the Fisher Committee on Abuse of Social Security Benefits, Cmnd. 5228 (1973).

Freedland: M.R. Freedland, Note on *Denmark Productions Ltd.* v. *Boscobel Productions Ltd.*, (1969) 32 M.L.R. 314.

Freeman: L.F. Freeman, "Able to Work and Available to Work," 55 Yale L.J. 123 (1945).

Fryer: R.H. Fryer, "Redundancy and Public Policy," in *Redundancy and Paternalist Capitalism* by R. Martin and R.H. Fryer (1973).

Grunfeld: C. Grunfeld, *The Law of Redundancy* (1971).

Haber and Murray: W. Haber and M.G. Murray, *Unemployment Insurance in the American Economy* (1966).

Handbook: Supplementary Benefits Handbook, Supplementary Benefit Administration Paper No.2, 4th ed., 1974.

Hauser and Burrows: M.M. Hauser and P. Burrows, *The The Economics of Unemployment Insurance* (1969).

Hepple and O'Higgins: B.A. Hepple and P. O'Higgins, *Individual Employment Law* (1971).

Jackson: D. Jackson, "Compensation for Loss of Pension Rights in Cases of Unfair Dismissal," (1975) 4 I.L.J. 24.

Kempfer: K. Kempfer, "Disqualification for Voluntary Leaving and Misconduct," 55 Yale L.J. 147 (1945).

Lynes: T. Lynes, *The Penguin Guide to Supplementary Benefits*, rev. ed. (1974).

Meacher: Molly Meacher, *Scrounging on the Welfare, the Scandal of the Four Week Rule* (1974).

Mesher: J. Mesher, "Earnings Related Benefits," (1974) 3 I.L.J. 118.

NEDC Report: National Economic Development Council, *Conditions Favourable to Faster Growth* (1963).

NJAC Report: Report of a National Joint Advisory Council Committee on Dismissals Procedures (1967).

Ogus: A.I. Ogus, "Unemployment Benefit for Workers on Short-Time," (1975) 4 I.L.J. 12.

Parker and Thomas: S.R. Parker and C.G. Thomas, *The Findings of the Survey, Effects of the Redundancy Payments Act*, Social Survey Division of Office of Population Censuses and Surveys (1971).

Phillips: Report of the Committee on Economic and Financial Problems of the Provision for Old Age, Cmd. 9333 (1954).

Report of the Government Actuary: Fourth Report of the Government Actuary on Occupational Pension Schemes (1971).

Richardson: J.H. Richardson, *Economic and Financial Aspects of Social Security* (1960).

Sanders: P.H. Sanders, "Disqualification for Unemployment Insurance," 8 Vand. L.R. 307 (1955).

Social Trends: Social Trends No. 3, Central Statistical Office (1972).

U.S. Dept. of Labor: *Unemployment Insurance : Purpose and Principles, Bureau of Employment Security,* U.S. Department of Labor (1950).

Wedderburn: K.W. Wedderburn, *The Worker and the Law,* 2nd ed. (1971).

INDEX